COMMUNICATING FINANCES IN THE FAMILY

Talking and Taking Action

COMMUNICATING FINANCES IN THE FAMILY

———— Talking and Taking Action ————

Roberta A. Davilla Robbins

Hawkeye Community College

A. Frank Thompson

University of Northern Iowa

cognella®

SAN DIEGO

Bassim Hamadeh, CEO and Publisher
Todd R. Armstrong, Publisher
Tony Paese, Project Editor
Alia Bales, Production Editor
Jess Estrella, Senior Graphic Designer
Trey Soto, Licensing Coordinator
Natalie Piccotti, Director of Marketing
Kassie Graves, Vice President of Editorial
Jamie Giganti, Director of Academic Publishing

Cover image:
Copyright © 2016 iStockphoto LP/sorbetto.
Copyright © 2018 iStockphoto LP/Oksana Latysheva.

Printed in the United States of America.

3970 Sorrento Valley Blvd., Ste. 500, San Diego, CA 92121

To the memory of my father, Robert H. "Bob" Davilla, who taught me early in life the difference between a "need" and a "want."

—RDR

To my parents, Walter, Martha, Andrew and Arlyne, my wife, Beth and daughter, Anne who taught me the importance and value of family communication when discussing finances.

—AFT

CONTENTS

Preface

"We were naïve about all things money."

This is a quotation by a mother on a television commercial advertising a credit union. The family depicted wanted to purchase a home. Thanks to the knowledge of the credit union employee, the family succeeded in their purchase.

Money is a fact of life. Everyone needs money to buy goods and services, pay bills, and save for "rainy days" and wealth building. Yet, like the mother expressed in the quote, many people are naïve about how to use money to create a comfortable life where their needs are met and their financial dreams become reality. Money is the means by which material goals are achieved. One of the purposes of this textbook is to help you move from seeing money as a "problem" to viewing money as the "path" to achieve your financial goals. The key to addressing financial issues is to have honest, fair, and helpful family discussions about finances. To this end, this book offers a communication framework for family conversations about finances.

As stated, the framework of the book emphasizes the relationship between communication and financial planning. The two parts of this framework include the financial communication process and the financial planning process. First, communication is recognized as a continuous process; its ubiquitous nature and function in our lives is explored by describing the communication process, key concepts, and strategies. Second, the financial planning process provides basic information to help families understand how to organize their money. The combination of these two processes makes this book unique. Most financial advice guidebooks emphasize the financial steps to creating wealth but infer the role of communication in this process. This book addresses how to communicate with your partner and family while making financial decisions. Particularly, the steps that you can take to better communicate with your partner and family when making financial decisions will be described. One of our purposes in this book is to help you understand how the tools of financial planning, along with the process of communication, can assist families to reach their financial goals to feel more secure and less stressed.

In addition to the economic reality of needing money, money also elicits emotions that range from stress and anxiety to fulfillment and feelings of reward. Personal reactions to the *meaning* of money come partly from family history, experiences using money, and individual feelings about it. Communication, or the lack of it, about money and financial decisions can have far-reaching consequences for couples and families. The ways in which couples and family members talk about how money will be used can influence the overall health of these important committed relationships.

The way parents, or primary caregivers, used and talked about money and made their financial decisions will influence how financial planning is embraced or avoided. Many people think that communication about finances begins between a committed couple. Yet, how the partners were raised to think about and discuss money can determine how well they communicate and make financial decisions. If the partners were given little direction about such issues as budgeting, saving, insurance, and retirement from their parents or primary caregivers, they may be at a loss to start a conversation about financial issues when establishing and maintaining their own committed relationship.

Often people avoid communicating about financial issues that require making difficult choices. This lack of communication can lead to great uncertainty. Not knowing leads a person to guess the reasons for choices that may be far from the truth and are shaded by personal perspectives on these matters. The decision not to communicate about finances leaves lasting impressions on committed and family relationships.

For example, communication within your original family about finances can influence your relationships with your parents, your siblings, and your partner. Let's say that, based on individual needs, your parents provided more financial assistance for one of your siblings than for the rest. It is not unusual that one child may have greater monetary need to achieve an educational, business, career, or personal goal than another child. This difference in financial assistance may lead to misunderstandings, hurt feelings, and long-term resentment between your family members, if the reasons for these decisions are not openly discussed. This situation can potentially influence your committed and current family relationships. This example, then, illustrates that the importance of the relationship between money and communication cannot be overstated. Nor should it be overlooked.

The purpose of *Communicating Finances in the Family: Talking and Taking Action* is to address the important relationship between communication and financial planning. The book will help couples and families think, talk, plan, and negotiate the use of their money. Most of the financial planning decisions faced by families are the result of family life stages, which include such events as entering into a committed relationship, having and caring for children, working, taking care of parents, securing retirement funds, and distributing wealth at the end of life. All of these family life stages require planning, budgeting, and, more importantly, communicating in order to reach these financial goals.

This book will appeal to many audiences because of its universal topic. A broad range of readers from undergraduate and graduate students to general interest readers will find relevance in this book. Readers who want to learn more about how to communicate with their partner and/or family about financial matters will particularly find the book helpful. As a standalone introduction to this issue, the book can be used as a supplementary or core reading in courses that focus on interpersonal communication, family communication, group communication, community, finance, and economics.

Communicating Finances in the Family: Talking and Taking Action is a breakthrough book because it is the first of its kind to merge communication with financial planning. Scholarly and popular literature emphasize the necessity for partners and families to discuss financial planning. Yet, theory-based communication is never revealed in these respective literatures. "Be sure to talk this over with your spouse or partner" is the general throw-away statement about the importance of communicating about financial matters. This book will have very broad appeal because of its timely and universally important topic.

A variety of special features are in this book. Learning objectives are listed at the beginning of each of the chapters. The objectives help the reader quickly see the information covered in the chapter and they function as an aid in quickly finding information. Case studies with discussion questions and sample responses are included in all six of the chapters. The case studies bring the terms and concepts discussed in the respective chapter "to life" to encourage immediate relevance and application to the reader's life situation.

Each chapter has ten true/false and multiple-choice questions and five essay questions for self-checks for the student/reader and potential test questions for faculty. These questions reinforce the terms, definitions, and applications introduced in each chapter. Self-check questions are good ways for both students, readers, and faculty to emphasize key communication and financial planning concepts.

Two "Consider This" examples, in chapters 1 and 3, request readers to stop and contemplate a financial situation and concept for further reflection. "Consider This" is application oriented to bring immediate relevance to your knowledge and experience in communication and financial planning. The reference section, end notes, and glossary at the end of the book provide resources and definitions for key terms used throughout the book.

The authors would like to thank their editorial team, Todd Armstrong and Tony Paese, along with the Cognella support teams for their assistance in the publication of this book. We are grateful that this project will see the light of day. We hope that you will find *Communicating Finances in the Family: Talking and Taking Action* helpful in meeting your family's financial planning needs through communication.

SECTION 1

THE BASICS

1

COMMUNICATION BASICS

LEARNING OBJECTIVES

After reading this chapter, you will be able to do the following:

1. Describe the nature of communication and some of our assumptions about it

2. Define family communication

3. Describe several communication terms: self-disclosure, conflict, family roles, family rules, and family life stages

4. Define the financial communication process

CASE STUDY 1

Christmas Comes Early to the Jones Household: Part I

Sally and Dave Jones live in Overland Park, Kansas, with their two children, Max (eight) and Audrey (five). Dave works as a software designer and communication specialist for a company that provides information technology solutions to doctors, hospitals, and clinics across the United States. He grew up in Hannibal, Missouri, where, as a high school student he mowed lawns, painted fences, and did odd jobs to save for college. Dave's father was a high school history teacher and his mother was an elementary school principal. In high school he began to enjoy studying and learning. His hard work, along with a curator's scholarship, allowed him to go to the University of Missouri. Graduating at the time of the 2008 recession, job interviews were scarce, but Dave was able to find employment where he had interned during college.

Sally also graduated from the University of Missouri with a degree in elementary education with reading and math specializations. She met Dave on the tennis courts, and it was a love match shortly thereafter. She grew up in a suburb outside of St. Louis. Remarkably, they were able to overlook their mixed loyalties in terms of baseball, getting married despite Dave being a Royals and Sally being a Cardinals fan. Sally obtained a third-grade teaching job close to their home.

Sally and Dave are avid gardeners. They share an interest in hiking with their children. Sally wants to instill in their children a love for books like her mother did for her. Sally's mother is a voracious reader but was unable to attend college due to the lack of funds. Sally's father founded a small plumbing business after working five years from apprentice to journeyman plumber. The plumbing business has been successful due to the commitment and hard work of Sally's parents. When Sally was born, her parents made a commitment to save enough money for her to attend college. All of Sally's college expenses were paid when she graduated. Additionally, Sally earned money for college during high school by babysitting and helping her father with bookkeeping for his business.

Dave and Sally attend church, are Sunday School teachers, and work with the church youth programs. They are committed to tithing, giving their time, and supporting causes that help feed the poor. They feel strongly about helping others.

Dave and Sally have noticed that Christmas items and decorations are appearing in stores much earlier than when they were growing up. The abundant lights, displays, and Santa Claus and holiday movies have also stimulated curiosity and excitement in their children about buying and receiving gifts. Sally has tried to use their interest to read and think about Christmas. She had Max read the **Polar Express** to Audrey and gave them an advent calendar so they can count the days and learn about Christian traditions.

Yet, Dave and Sally have found it challenging to keep their children focused on something other than the commercial sales view of Christmas (Hudson). Both children have made brief Christmas lists. Max has listed a 15-speed mountain bike ($350), Holy Stone drone with a video camera ($250), and an Apple iPad ($350). Audrey listed a Fisca remote-controlled dog ($90), an American Girl Wellie Wishers Camille doll ($60), a Power TRC super market sweet shop and ice cream cart ($25), and a Kidkraft Chelsea doll cottage with furniture ($62). Sally suspects that Max may have put Audrey up to requesting her first item. She wonders if it should be purchased as a common gift to share.

For the past four weeks Audrey has daily asked her parents when Christmas will come so that she can receive her gifts. Sally and Dave are planning to discuss with their children Christmas gift giving and ways to celebrate without making large gift expenditures. As you read chapter 1, consider how Sally and Dave can use the concepts and processes to help them during their family "talk."

THE NATURE OF COMMUNICATION

Communication is essential to our daily lives. We talk, listen, and text, among many other activities. Yet, communication is often misunderstood. People sometimes think that because they have "communicated" throughout their entire lives, that they are good at it. This is not always so. Communication as an activity can be refined and improved on no matter how good a communicator we think that we might be. Within this context, some may believe they are fully communicating about finances to family members, but there will always be opportunities to improve the discussion. The financial planning process presented in the next chapter highlights how this improvement mechanism works to incrementally benefit decision making.

Let's first consider the nature of communication and some of our assumptions about it.

Communication means to make common or to build community. Communication is based on two Latin words, *communis* and *communicare*. *Communis* is a noun that means common or sharing. *Communicare* is a verb that means "to make something common" (Nepal). **Communication** is a complex process through which we symbolically create and share messages and meanings with others. Communication is symbolic because we use words and nonverbal cues to express a range of thoughts and feelings. For example, families may have a habit of ending phone calls with "I love you" to signal their mutual affection. If the phrase is not said, this may mean a hidden conflict or that a third party is present who is making the intimate expression inappropriate. In the financial planning process, clarifying what you mean as "wealth" or having "a lot of money" will be necessary so that the family will understand the meaning of these terms. Having a common understanding of the symbols that we use will help avoid misunderstandings.

A significant study that was published in 1967 is still considered the foundation for understanding communication and interpersonal relationships. *Pragmatics of Human Communication* by Paul Watzlawick, Janet Beavin Bavelas, and Don D. Jackson presented five principles that continue to influence our understanding of communication.

- People cannot *not* communicate. Everything that we do and say (or not say) communicates a message to other people.
- Every communication interaction has a content and a relational part. The content is *what* we say; the relational part is *how* we say

it. We may share information (content), but we also express how we feel about the relationship (relational).

- The relationship between two people is *punctuated* in their interactions. Each person thinks that his or her communication is a reaction to (or caused by) the other person's behavior.
- Human communication consists of both verbal and nonverbal components.
- All communication interactions are *symmetrical* (based on equal power between the communicators) or *complementary* (based on power differences between the communicators).

These five principles have guided our understanding of communication by being reinforced, debated, and extended by interpersonal communication scholars. (See Verderber, Sellnow, & Verderber, 2017 for additional interpersonal communication concepts and topics.)

FAMILY COMMUNICATION

Families are one of the settings for communication. Families, by definition, can be based on biological ties or can be ties of the heart. The contemporary definition of a "family" is becoming less about biology and more about emotional connections. For our purposes in this book, a **family** can range from a couple to multi-generations who live together and function to collectively create a stable, safe, and satisfying environment for its members. Family members have something in common: to function as a group. "Family" is formed by and through communication.

No two families are alike. Yet, being a member of a family is a universal experience. We spend our lives entering, creating, maintaining, and sometimes leaving a family. Our sense of family is a unique communication process. Our personal identities, roles, and understandings of what it is to be a part of a family are constructed and experienced by our interactions with other family members. In a real sense, our view and understanding of the world are largely the result of our early and growing up years spent in our original family. (See Galvin, Braithwaite, Schrodt, & Bylund, 2019 among other family communication textbooks for more family communication concepts.)

To begin to unpack the role of communication in family interactions, the basic concepts of the financial communication process will be developed. The financial communication process will provide the basis for the financial planning process, which will provide the specifics for developing a family's short, intermediate, and long-term financial goals.

Several communication terms will be briefly described and illustrated. All of the terms could be considerably developed. If you would like to know more, there are numerous interpersonal communication books available to consult, as well as referring to the references noted. For our purposes in this book, we are specifically applying these terms and concepts to the topic of communicating about money and financial planning. Let's begin by discussing an important interpersonal communication concept, self-disclosure.

Self-Disclosure

Self-disclosure is revealing information to another person that he or she would not otherwise know. (See Derlega, Metts, Petronio, & Margulis, 1993 among other researchers who study self-disclosure). Suffice it to say that self-disclosure can be risky business. Self-disclosure takes place by the level of risk involved. The three levels of risk are low, middle, and high.

Low level self-disclosure provides minimal risk to the person saying something about him- or herself. For example, when you meet a new person, telling your name and hometown are generally considered low risk. Students new to a class may participate in an "ice breaker" activity that allows the instructor and the students to become acquainted. Responding to such questions as your year in school, major, hometown, and expectations for the class would most likely not conjure feelings of risk in disclosing this information to others in the class. In a family, telling your sibling your favorite color or ice cream flavor would be most likely a low-risk self-disclosure.

Mid-level self-disclosure inches up the risk category. Talking about your likes, dislikes, and feelings is mid-level disclosures. When we talk about our thoughts and opinions regarding current news stories, our income tax bill, and political parties we are risking a negative reaction to our thoughts and opinions. We risk being negatively evaluated by the person because of the thoughts and opinions we hold. Friendships are based on feeling "safe" to discuss our likes, dislikes, and feelings. Friends do not necessarily have to hold the same attitudes, values, and opinions. Yet, the friendship is one of the "safe" zones where we can discuss differences of opinion and not feel that the friendship is at risk.

High-level self-disclosure is when we feel the greatest risk in telling information about ourselves. The negative evaluation of ourselves by the other person is at its greatest possibility. Secrets and difficult past experiences are examples of high-level self-disclosure. Telling another person about our near-death experience or our belief in angels potentially creates high risk for negative evaluation.

Our thoughts and attitudes about money are mid- to high-level risk topics. For example, if a family has experienced bankruptcy or severe financial struggles, disclosing this information to another can raise questions about the family's ability to handle money successfully. Our willingness to self-disclose our attitudes, values, and beliefs about money is an important factor in the financial communication process that will be more fully described later in this chapter.

There may be different layers to self-disclosure, particularly when dealing with finances. In some public settings, a discussion of rudimentary finances may be shared between friends, neighbors, or relatives on a need-to-know basis. So, if a truck arrives at your home, and a couple of burly men off-load a baby grand piano into your living room, a neighbor, who has a daughter interested in music lessons, may ask where you purchased the instrument, how you decided on that model, and how much it cost.

At a family reunion, you may have a private discussion with a sister-in-law about one of your nephews who is going off to college. She may volunteer that despite having received an academic scholarship, next year's tuition will be $25,000 and they are wondering where the money will come from. In the course of any conversation about money and finances, it may be prudent to ascertain from all parties the confidentiality of such discussions. Yet, self-disclosure is an important concept to consider in the family communication process. Let's now take up the inevitable reality of interpersonal conflict.

Interpersonal Conflict

Conflict is an inevitable reality of life. Whenever there are two people, there is potential for conflict to arise. Finding a seat on the bus can create conflict because of the limited number of seats on the bus.

An academic definition of interpersonal conflict can be found in Joyce L. Hocker and William W. Wilmot's *Interpersonal Conflict* textbook. **Interpersonal conflict** is an expressed struggle between at least two inter-dependent parties who perceive incompatible goals, scarce resources, and interference from others in achieving their goals. Wow! What a definition! Let's try to break this down to help us understand conflict.

An expressed struggle means that conflict has to be spoken. We can't hide behind conflict; it has to be expressed through talk. Ever fume about something? Did it help to keep it inside? Probably not. Talk has to be a part of the conflict process.

Two interdependent parties are people who depend on each other. In families, children depend on their parents to provide them with food, shelter, and clothing as basic needs. Parents depend on their children to follow rules, go to school, show respect, and help around the house, among other things. In other words, families depend on each other and are, thus, interdependent.

The perception of incompatible goals can be a range of things such as which restaurant you are going to eat before you go to the movie on Friday night. There are only so many restaurants and so many movies at any given time from which to select. You may want to go for pizza, but another family member may want to eat Asian. You might want to see the latest action movie while another family member may want to see a romantic comedy.

Another example of incompatible goals that families may experience are where to go on vacation and when. Busy schedules may influence the length of time for the family vacation and distance away from home.

One family member may have a particular talent that the entire family participates in such as car racing. One family member may be the actual driver, but the entire family is expected to go to the weekend races and participate in the event. The expectation becomes what the family "does together." As resident children grow and mature, they may no longer want to participate in the family race car weekends. Conflict may arise because the family identity begins to erode and the group outings begin to pass away from the entire family experience.

Scarce resources can be time, money, and opportunities for advancement, to name a few. For our purposes in this book, we will focus on the scarce or finite resource of money. If a family is stressed over what they perceive as the lack of money, the competing goals of individual family members on how to use the resource available can lead to conflict. Of course, many families do experience lack of funds to meet their goals of providing for the family.

Interference from others can be people who are outside the immediate family or another outside source who either implicitly or explicitly put pressure on the family to do, think, or believe in a way that is counter to the established family values, beliefs, and goals. For example, an in-law may complain about the rest of the family not being about to spend holidays together. The family feels guilty and stressed about not being able to comply or participate to the degree expected. A family member may join a political party or faith-based group or have a particular entertainment preference that counters the values, attitudes, and beliefs of the rest of the family.

One family member may receive financial assistance from a parent or a grandparent who recognizes a particular need that would help one of their children or grandchildren succeed. If this type of financial help is kept hidden without explanation, hurt feelings and conflict could ensue once the facts become known within the family. Often in the case of a family business, there can be differences between family members on who will eventually run the firm after the death of their parents. If parents fail to openly discuss the issue of family succession within their business, it will likely lead to conflict between brothers and sisters over leadership. Often, these conflicts arise after the death of parents when there is no way to know their wishes on this issue of succession.

Differences of opinion can be a major cause of conflict within families. These pressures can contribute to obstacles in the family financial planning process because of competing interests coupled with finite resources, in this case, money.

In sum, conflict can be caused by differences of opinion and goals; limited resources, such as time and money; or a third person muscling in on your relationship. When we talk about the points of disagreement or worry, conflict management or resolution begins. Conflict is not intended to be violent, although unfortunately, it can be reduced to violence. For our purposes, conflict episodes will occur in respectful and nonviolent manners. With respect to finances, the financial planning process is designed to promote family financial communication, leading to respectful discussion and resolution of financial matters.

CONSIDER THIS

Do not underestimate the powerful impact expectations can have on family financial communication and future decision making. Suppose a couple, at the time of their marriage, agrees to try to see each set of in-laws for the holidays every other year. One year will be with one set of in-laws, the next year with the other in-laws. They have created an expectation that efforts will be made for holiday visits between both sets of parents throughout their marriage. Initially this open-ended commitment may be easier to perform without children. However, with each passing year, this couple is establishing an expectation in the minds of their parents that some part of the holidays will be spent with them and their grandchildren. As a consequence, despite the cost of traveling to and from their extended families during the winter, they continue to meet this expectation. However, as time goes on, and with the addition of children, this couple begins to re-evaluate this tradition. What about holiday traditions within their own family? What happens if the couple moves many miles away from one set of in-laws? What about issues related to weather and travel costs in the time period before and after the holidays? What if the children want to spend the holidays closer to their friends, particularly during the middle school and high school years? This issue illustrates how family commitments can sometimes entail financial obligations, based on expectations, that need to be discussed with extended family members. Avoiding such a conversation because it may be difficult will not lead to family peace and harmony, but could lead to resentment. The couple really does not know how their in-laws may feel about their staying home for the holidays unless the subject is broached and the reasons, financial and child-rearing related, are discussed.

Family Roles

The idea of roles existing in families provokes considerable disagreement among role theorists and communication scholars (Galvin). For our purposes, **family roles** are similar to roles that actors play in a theatrical production. Roles are communicatively created. In other words, the roles that each family develop and enact are created through the communication interactions within the family. Family roles can change, emerge, pass away, and be rejected. The McMaster model of family functioning (Epstein et.al., 581) is helpful in describing how families assign responsibilities and manage answerability for them. The McMaster model views the family like a mobile. A mobile has separate parts but hangs together as it moves through space. Five essential family functions are the foundation for family roles. The five essential areas are providing for

1. provision of resources;
2. nurturance and support;
3. adult sexual gratification;

4. personal development;

5. maintenance and management of the family system (Epstein et al., 591).

Given these areas, the financial planning process falls within the family management area. We could extend our examination of family roles to describe the types of wage earners that are within families, such as single-career, dual-career, teenage workers, and retired but still working categories. For the purposes of the financial communication process and the financial planning process, we level the field by looking at the entire financial outcome rather than at the individual earners who contribute to this outcome. The following example illustrates how family roles can shift and change.

As parents become elderly, the family role of caregiver can shift from the parent to the now adult-child because of the elderly parent's physical and cognitive limitations. Financial discussions about money, which may have previously been forbidden in families, are now front and center as a family need. If the family rule was to prevent children from being present during financial discussions or that children should not be aware of the family's financial stability, then the financial discussion between the now elderly parent and adult-child may be quite difficult.

In some cases, the financial discussion may not occur between the elderly parent and adult-child. Instead, the adult-child may discover the financial status of the parent through a discussion with bank officers, financial planners, lawyers, and health care providers. These roles spill out of the immediate family and become known to the community in which the family lives, at least in general terms.

Roles are behaviors that become consistent with the needs of the family. As we saw in the previous example, the roles between the parent and child have shifted and changed significantly to meet the family need for providing care and resources for the now elderly parent. Let's consider this movement from another time. For instance, parents of young families are typically grownups who have children. As the adults and parents, their roles are to provide food, shelter, clothing, and a sense of security to their children, which includes physical, emotional, and sometimes spiritual safety.

Children, on the other hand, because they require physical and emotional care and are economically dependent, cannot care for themselves. Part of their role is to go to school to learn socially agreed-on values for education and to prepare for adulthood. As children become teenagers and young adults, their abilities and roles become more independent and self-sufficient as they navigate toward adulthood. Conflict can be plentiful during the teenage years because learning independence and life away from the family can create tension.

Some teens may have jobs. Jobs create individual economic resources and wealth. In our Western and capitalist society, economic wealth is closely related to power and the luxury of personal decision making. As teens enter early adulthood, the questions are, "How much financial independence should parents relinquish to their children? What happens when a teenager's job-related activities take away time and focus from educational pursuits and accomplishment?" Differences of opinion and conflict can arise as the family roles, and the expectations that we have of ourselves in our family role, shift and change. Those differences may relate to how the parents were raised in terms of the degree of independence, restrictions, and support they were given with respect to activities.

In 2006, authors Graham Allan and Christian Gerstner asserted that the very nature of money has issues of power and dependency. They suggest that during a monetary exchange the material or nonmaterial goods are transacted and the meaning of the transaction is understood by the participants. For example, when shopping for groceries, the buyer pays for the groceries with currency (cash or credit card). The cashier accepts the currency as payment in full for the groceries. Each participant is satisfied that the completed exchange of groceries for payment has occurred.

Money becomes not only the means to purchase goods and services, but it takes on social meanings that are culturally "situated" and understood. The cultural situatedness reflects the gendered nature as well as other social meanings of power and dependency. For instance, in previous generations, the purchase of groceries was generally considered the responsibility of females in the family, such as the wife or grandmother. Men provided the currency for the purchase of the groceries through their work. Yet, the domain of the grocery store was sometimes viewed as a primarily feminine location where females were more often the customers. This attitude has changed. A grocery store today is not considered a necessarily gendered location because the view now is that everyone can and needs to buy groceries. The reasons for this shift are beyond the scope of this book.

The cultural, gendered, and age-related nature of monetary transactions is an expansive topic. Children's dependency and their respective gender will influence their parents' view of their own economic power and that of their children. As children become teenagers or young adults with jobs, they become less economically dependent on their parents' provision for economic needs. Parents, whether by agreement or conflict, will need to evaluate their own relinquishment of power over their children's now growing economic independence. To suggest that there may be discrimination or oppression in these choices raises philosophical understandings that are a part of our own family identities, social status, and economic positions. The purpose of this book is to acknowledge these disparities while at the same time practically address how a family will work through their cultural, gendered, and age-related situatedness to accomplish their financial goals.

Family Rules

Family rules are guidelines for living as a family (See Shimanoff, 1980). Rules are the frameworks for helping a family function in the day-to-day activities that reveal themselves through appropriate and expected behaviors, meal times, chores, and exhibiting respectful behavior. Routine tasks such as cleaning, laundry, caring for pets, and family entertainment activities are just a few of the areas where a family's implicit or explicit rules are experienced.

An implicit rule is one that is not spoken. For example, dining etiquette or not sneaking out of the house after everyone has gone to bed are implicit rules. We may have instruction on how to eat with a fork, which spoon to use, and to indicate that you have finished our meal by placing your utensils on your plate. The instruction is making the "rule" explicit. From then on, however, if we do not demonstrate what we have learned from the training, we are violating the implicit rule of showing good manners by using them in dining situations. Likewise, families may have not overtly stated that children and teenagers should not sneak out of the house after everyone has retired for the night. Yet, if a child or teenager does so, the implicit rule of not sneaking out of the house becomes a problem. The "rule" has been violated and there will be consequences or punishment because the child or teen has violated the implicit rule.

An explicit rule is one that is spoken. Telling family members that they need to attend a worship service together or when mealtime will begin is stating the rule for the respective situation. If family members are late or a no-show, then the explicit "rule" has been broken.

Family roles and rules are important concepts in helping families navigate necessary day-to-day activities and their fulfillment. Let's move on to the area of family dynamics and how they are defined and communicatively used for yet another area of family functioning.

Family Dynamics

Cohesion, adaptability, and communication are three dimensions that have been frequently studied in marital and family interactions. Olson, Sprenkle, and Russell (3) developed what is known as the Circumplex Model. Researchers, including Carnes (1989), have used this model for research, clinical diagnoses, and as a teaching tool. **Cohesion** is the emotional bonds that families have. **Adaptability** is the ability to adjust to ever-changing family circumstances and experiences. Communication is the process by which cohesion and adaptability are expressed.

Cohesion can be represented on a straight line. The left arrow represents low cohesion; the right arrow refers to high cohesion. Cohesion is described as four levels extending from one end to the other (108).

FIGURE 1.1 Cohesion

Disengaged families	Separated families	Connected families	Enmeshed families
← Low			High →

Source: Patrick Carnes, "Cohesion," *Contrary to Love: Helping the Sexual Addict.* CompCare Publications, 1989.

Disengaged: Families are very separate and have little sense of loyalty or family belonging.

Separated: Families have emotional independence but do have some sense of loyalty and family belonging.

Connected: Families seek emotional closeness, loyalty, and joint involvement yet they like some individuality.

Enmeshed: Families seek extreme closeness and loyalty and do not experience individuality.

For example, a family that rarely talks or sees each other would be considered a *disengaged* family. Little communication exists between and among the family members, so little loyalty and a sense of family belonging happen. On the opposite end, a family that does everything together such as take vacations, have family-only picnics and other exclusive family social activities, and even live in close proximity would be considered *enmeshed* families. Interaction and activities are primarily with and among the defined family. Outside friends and acquaintances remain just that, outside the family. *Separated* families can be thought of as relatively independent in terms of interacting with the family. Friendships and acquaintances are created and maintained with people outside the family. A wide circle of friends can exist. Yet, the family members still have a sense of knowing that they belong and appreciate that they are a part of their family. Finally, the *connected* family prefers feeling emotionally close with frequent family activities and interactions. Having a sense of personal identity and independence does not disrupt the family. Both closeness with the family and personal independence are balanced.

A second concept that is important to thinking about the family system has to do with adaptability. Similar to cohesion, adaptability, also called flexibility, has four levels from low to high (Carnes, 105).

FIGURE 1.2 Adaptability

Rigid families	Structured families	Flexible families	Chaotic families

Low   High

Source: Fig. 1.2: Patrick Carnes, "Adaptabiility," *Contrary to Love: Helping the Sexual Addict*. Comp-Care Publications, 1989.

Rigid:	Families function with autocratic decision making with strict roles and rules.
Structured:	Families function with authoritarian or occasional equalitarian decision making with stable roles and rules.
Flexible:	Families function with negotiation in decision making with roles and rules that are easily changed.
Chaotic:	Families function without leadership, muddled decision making, and mixed roles and rules.

Rigid families have very clearly defined roles, boundaries, and decision-making rules. Presumably the parents would be the decision makers, with little to no input from children or other extended family members. Clearly defined roles and rules about how the family conducts itself would also exist. Every family member knows his or her place and responsibility. The family system, though, is so closed that new ideas and adapting to expanding habits are not appreciated or allowed to enter the family system. *Structured* families are slightly more adaptable with clearly defined roles and rules but occasionally will entertain new ideas and habits in terms of decision making and creating an openness to new ways of doing things. *Flexible* families encourage negotiation and have roles and rules that can change. If a chore needs to be completed, it does not fall to one family member because of his or her role to do the task. The task completion becomes more important than the particular family member who does it. Household chores, outdoor lawn maintenance, and other domestic responsibilities are everyone's responsibility, not just one person's role venue. *Chaotic* families are so adaptable that much confusion exists about who is in charge of what and how the roles and rules will be applied and accomplished. No leadership exists and a sense of structure in daily living for the family is not evident. Chaotic families have no rules or defined roles.

Cohesion and adaptability are frequently represented together in a two-axes diagram: One axis is horizontal; the other axis vertical. The central point on the axes signifies the balance of cohesion and adaptability (see figure 1.3).

FIGURE 1.3 Family Cohesion-Adaptability Axes

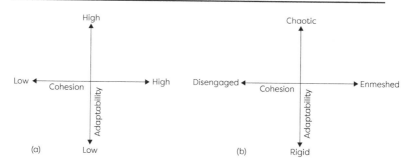

Source: Patrick Carnes, "Family Cohesion-Adaptability Axes," *Contrary to Love: Helping the Sexual Addict.* CompCare Publications, 1989.

The utility for this model is that it shows and describes how families can shift and change based on family behaviors and circumstances.

The concepts of cohesion and adaptability and their respective levels enable us to see how individual members' thinking, feelings, and abilities influence the entire family system. For instance, if one parent or child is more independent and disconnected from the entire family than the other parent or other children, this emotional distance will influence how the family makes decisions about routine activities as well as financial planning. These behaviors and attitudes reflect the overall cohesion of the family.

Likewise, the family's ability to adapt to day-to-day and life changes will be reflected in its overall coping. If family members have varying levels of adaptability, one member will be less troubled with change than another. The collective family adaptability measure will influence how the family copes as a whole to the change before them.

For the purposes of this book, the two mid-levels are in our writing assumptions. A balance of cohesion and adaptability is needed to achieve the conversations, conflict management, and decision making to complete the various steps in the financial communication and financial planning processes.

FAMILY LIFE-CYCLE STAGES

The stages of the family life cycle model, created by Monica McGoldrick, Betty Carter, and Nydia Garcia Preto, is one way to see the developmental trajectory of families (2). At its center is the importance of communication at all stages of the life cycles and thus gives us much utility in considering the stages of a family's life. This model has its limitations because it normalizes the two-parent with children family. It also presumes the natural order progression of life, such as parents passing away before younger family members. Not all unexpected crises faced by families may be accounted for in this model. Table 1.1 is an adaptation of the model. "Being born" and "death" stages are added to broaden the life stages and the financial responsibilities and challenges that accompany these life cycle stages. We will refer to the stages of the family life cycle as various financial planning documents are created.

TABLE 1.1 Adaptation of the Stages of the Family Life Cycle

Family life cycle stage	Emotional process of transition: Key principles	Second-order changes in the family status required to proceed developmentally
Being born	Dependence on parental support and nurture	a. Developing bonds with parents b. Establishing caregiver connection with parents
Emerging young adults	Accepting emotional and financial responsibility for self	a. Differentiation of self in relation to family of origin b. Development of intimate peer relationships c. Establishment of self in respect to work and financial independence d. Establishment of self in community and larger society e. Establishment of one's worldview, spirituality, religion, and relationship to nature f. Parents shifting to consultative role in young adult's relationships

Family life cycle stage	Emotional process of transition: Key principles	Second-order changes in the family status required to proceed developmentally
Couple formation: The joining of families through commitment, union, or marriage	Commitment to new system	a. Formation of committed system b. Realignment of relationships with extended families and friends to include spouse/partner c. Realignment of relationships among couple, parents and siblings, extended family, friends, and larger community
Families with young children	Accepting new members into the system	a. Adjustment of committed system to make space for children b. Collaboration in child rearing and financial and household tasks c. Realignment of relationships with extended family to include parenting and grandparenting roles d. Realignment of relationships with community and larger social system to include new family structure and relationships
Families with adolescents	Increasing flexibility of family boundaries to permit children's independence and grandparents' families	a. Shifting of parent-child relationships to permit adolescent to have more independent activities and relationships and to move more flexibly in and out of the system b. Families helping emerging adolescents negotiate relationships with community c. Refocus on midlife couple and career issues d. Beginning to shift toward caring for older generation
Launching children and moving on at midlife	Accepting a multitude of exits from and entries into the system	a. Renegotiation of couple system as a dyad b. Development of adult-to-adult relationships between parents and grown-up children c. Realignment of relationships to include in-laws and grandchildren d. Realignment of relationships with community to include new constellation of family relationships e. Exploration of new interests/career, given the freedom from child care responsibilities d. Dealing with health needs, disabilities, and death of parents (grandparents)

(continued)

TABLE 1.1 Adaptation of the Stages of the Family Life Cycle (*Cont.*)

Family life cycle stage	Emotional process of transition: Key principles	Second-order changes in the family status required to proceed developmentally
Families in late middle age	Accepting shifting generational roles	a. Maintaining or modifying own and/or couple social functioning and interests in the face of physiological decline; exploration of new familial and social role options b. Supporting more central role of middle generations c. Making room in the system for the wisdom and experience of the elders d. Supporting older generation without over-functioning for them
Families nearing the end of life	Accepting the realities of family members' limitations and death and the completion of one cycle of life	a. Dealing with loss of spouse/partner, siblings, and other peers b. Making preparation for death and legacy c. Managing reversed roles in caretaking between middle and older generations d. Realignment of relationships with larger community and social system to acknowledge changing life-cycle relationships e. Deciding on type and extent of care for terminal illness
Death	Life ends	a. Survivors make final arrangements or implement the pre-arrangement wishes b. Survivors handle legal and probate issues in settling the estate c. Survivors grieve the loss of their loved ones in the circle of life

Source: Adapted from Monica McGoldrick, Betty A. Carter, and Nydia A. Garcia Preto, "The Stages of the Family Life Cycle," *The Expanding Family Life Cycle: Individual, Family, and Social Perspectives*, p. 2. Pearson Education, Inc., 2016.

FINANCIAL COMMUNICATION PROCESS

There is no such thing as a "normal" family. Instead, family communication scholars speak in terms of functioning. Instead of asking ourselves, "How does my family measure up against my friends' and other people's?"

Ask, "How can my family optimize satisfaction between/among us?" "How can my family overcome dysfunctional behaviors so that we can minimize anxiety and create more stability among us?" Satisfaction/dissatisfaction and stability/insecurity are better measures of how your particular family functions instead of thinking, "Are we normal?"

The social comparison that often arises when talking about our families may also relate to our family's sense of financial well-being. Thinking about how our family's financial situation and status "measure up" to other families is unfair. The purpose of this book is to help all families achieve their idiosyncratic and unique financial plans. Let's go back a few steps.

One basic assumption that the authors have is that we value talk. Our hope by now is that you are beginning to see how communication is central to families, generally, and to the process of family financial planning, specifically. The overlay of several factors, family roles, rules, feelings of cohesion, and the ability to adapt, are at work within the stages of the family life cycle. These are communication activities that help families achieve their instrumental goals of family continuity (routine daily tasks) along with the leadership and emotional support that are expected within a family by parents and among family members.

Second, disclosure about our points of disagreement are important to approaching and clarifying our goals. These can be any goals, personal or family, such as borrowing the car to meet friends on a Friday night or where the family will vacation. As long as two people exist, conflict will occur. The collective goal of a family requires disclosure so that views and feelings can be expressed in a respectful and supportive environment. Even with age disparity between parents and children, the presence of power by parents over children does not need to adversely affect effective instruction about money. Learning the difference between a need and a want can help children see how money is a path for achieving a goal. Finally, disclosure is key to the financial communication process. Before effective financial planning can occur, disclosure and conflict management are necessary so that a like-minded choice can be put forward.

Ultimately, the financial communication process in the context of financial planning requires a decision. Our location of cohesion and adaptability on their respective continua influence the family's decision-making process. If your family is highly enmeshed, you may feel implicit pressure to agree with the more powerful family members. A disconnected family may not have the inclination to express their opinions to achieve a decision.

Decision making is a communication process. In 1970 R. H. Turner identified three levels of agreement: consensus, accommodation, and *de facto.* Each level reflects varying acceptance and commitment by the family. Let's consider each level of agreement.

Consensus is the most discussion-based level of agreement. It is also considered the most democratic. The expectation is that all participants in the discussion will talk about their opinions and areas of agreement and disagreement. Consensus building is very time consuming with the assumption that discussion will continue until all members agree on the decision. Considerable "buy in" is a benefit of this style of decision making because commitment to the agreement has been achieved presumably through the talk.

Accommodation is basically letting others make the decision because discussion or continuing discussion is viewed as having no effect on the ultimate agreement. Issues of power imbalance and lack of commitment to the decision are emphasized in the accommodation level of agreement. A domineering person may implicitly pressure the other family members into following along with the decision. Even if a vote is taken to give the appearance of a democratic process, winners and losers become more obvious. The losers are identified and the winners appear in control.

De facto decisions occur when an impasse has occurred. No clear agreement has been achieved through talking. In this case, a family member makes the decision so that the family can move on. This level of agreement seems very practical, yet family members have no commitment to the *de facto* decision and are more likely to complain about it.

Just as in other groups, families develop a "style" of decision making. The style or habits developed go back to the issues of cohesion and adaptability that were discussed earlier. If you are part of a family that is rigid in adaptability, asking for a family discussion to talk about a decision may be very threatening to the family member or members who usually make the decision without question. The phases of decision making illustrated in the problem-solving loop provide a process by which discussion-based decisions occur.

Talking is at the core of the financial communication process. **The family problem-solving loop** developed by Kieren, Maguire & Hurlbut in 1996, is intended as a guide to help families identify when disclosure (the "talking" part) and the decision (the "action" part) come together. The loop assists families in using talk to move from money as a problem to a path for their financial goals. We recognize that the problem-solving loop is our theoretical ideal and not necessarily reflective of what actually happens during discussions. It's a guide, not an assurance, for disclosure and decision making.

For our purposes, let's consider the eight steps of the loop, remembering that the ribbon is the symbol for talk.

Phase 1 (steps 1–3) is where the problem is identified, a goal is stated, and the current resources are calculated.

Phase 2 (steps 4 and 5) incorporates talking about alternatives and considering the pros and cons of them.

Phase 3 (step 6) could be the lengthiest phase because this is where the "best" alternative is decided. Anticipate extensive discussion and disclosure in this phase because a decision will ultimately need to be made and supported. Conflict may erupt in this phase as differing opinions about resources or the lack of them could be expressed.

Phase 4 (steps 7 and 8) is when the decision is put into place and evaluated at a later time. The evaluation of the decision is a mindful activity because talking about the outcome of the decision can be forgotten. Disclosure about the outcome is a good follow-up and reminder of the value of the loop to help families solve their financial goals and problems.

With each discussion and decision that needs to be made, think about the problem-solving loop and how it can guide your family's disclosure and decision-making sessions.

FIGURE 1.4 The Family Problem-Solving Loop

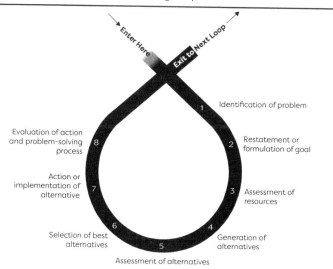

Source: Kathleen M. Galvin, et al., from "The Family Problem-Solving Loop," *Family Communication: Cohesion and Change*. Routledge, 2018.

CHAPTER SUMMARY

Chapter 1 introduced you to the nature of communication and some of our assumptions about it. Family communication was defined and the communication terms, self-disclosure, conflict, family roles, family rules, family dynamics, and family life stages, were defined and demonstrated. The financial communication process was described and illustrated.

SAMPLE RESPONSE TO CASE STUDY 1
Christmas Comes Early to the Jones Household: Part I

Identify and describe the family communication issues and methods for developing a healthy conversation on this topic.

Dave and Sally's family backgrounds demonstrate a commitment to earning and saving money through hard work to attain goods, services, and goals. Their participation in church and Sunday School is important to them as a family. Sally indicates an interest in using their time and talents to benefit others rather than thinking only of themselves.

How can they approach the topic of Christmas giving with a discussion of gift expenditures that will be consistent with their values?

Sally and Dave need to select a time and place for having a family meeting about Christmas gift giving. Weekday evenings might be a possibility, but work schedules, meal preparation, and after-school activities would need to be taken into consideration. A meeting during the weekend, perhaps Sunday afternoon, might pose fewer scheduling conflicts with fewer distractions. Sally and Dave need to agree on the amount of time and strategies needed to fully cover this family communication topic. They might set aside 30 to 40 minutes given their children's ages. In preparation for their gathering, Sally and Dave could complete Internet research on materials and strategies that might make learning about wants and needs entertaining and educational (Morin). They might also discuss this issue with ministers and Sunday School coworkers to learn of materials to present that are consistent with their beliefs. One idea might be to collect items within their home and have Max and Audrey guess which item is a want or need. A chart could be developed by putting two columns on a sheet of paper with one labeled "Needs" the other "Wants." As each item gets added to the list, a description could be included as to why it is a want or a need.

With the next trip to the grocery or shopping mall, Sally or Dave could ask their children to identify three wants and three needs in the store. By making differences between wants and needs into a game, Sally and Dave can reinforce the concept and add some fun to learning a key financial concept. Prior to their meeting they could also investigate movies that might provide an alternative to the commercial view of Christmas. Some possibilities might be *The Muppet Christmas Carol,* Dr. Seuss's *How the Grinch Stole Christmas, I Want a Dog for Christmas, Charlie Brown,* and/or *A Charlie Brown Christmas.* If time permits, they could also introduce the connection between payment for wants and needs within the family budget.

Learning the importance of funding needs first is important to the concept of budgeting later on. As a way of introducing this idea, Dave and Sally could use a trip to the grocery store to test Max and Audrey's understanding of a want versus a need. Each child could be given a small budget, such as $5, to purchase one gift for someone else. After buying these gifts, Dave and Sally could help their children determine who would receive the gifts, such as a friend, favorite teacher, or a charitable organization.

SELF-CHECK QUESTIONS

True/False

1. Communication is a complex process through which people symbolically create and share messages and meanings with others.
2. Some people cannot communicate, and every communication has a content and irrational component.
3. Self-disclosure involves revealing information to another person that she or he would not otherwise know.
4. High-level self-disclosure provides minimal risk to the person saying something about themselves.
5. Conflict represents struggle between at least two interdependent parties who perceive incompatible goals, scarce resources, and interference from others in achieving their goals.
6. A difference of opinion between a couple over the purchase of a Honda SUV versus a Lexus sedan is an example of the perception of incompatible goals within a family.

7. Money in exchange to purchase goods or services can take on social meanings that are culturally situated and understood, such as a young adults' desire for independence but need for family funds to help pay for college.

8. Family financial planning decisions are the result of family life stages, which include entering committed relationships, having and caring for children, working, taking care of parents, securing retirement funds, and distributing wealth at the end of life.

9. Family roles are likened to parts played by actors in a production.

10. The problem-solving loop is intended as a guide to help families identify when disclosure (the "talking" part) and the decision (the "action" part) come together in the financial communication process.

Multiple-Choice Questions

1. Which of the following basic principles influence our understanding of communication?
   a. Every communication interaction has a content and relational part
   b. The relationship between two people is punctuated during their interactions
   c. Communication is digital based on spoken words
   d. All of the above
   e. Only a and b

2. An expressed conflict is
   a. one that may only be conveyed in writing.
   b. one that involves two independent parties.
   c. one that involves those with compatible views.
   d. one that is spoken and expressed by talking.
   e. requires that a power difference exists between the participants.

3. High-level self-disclosure
   a. involves minimal risk because it is between two wealthy individuals.
   b. is characterized by talking about our thoughts and opinions about current sports news.

   c. has great risk because it involves telling information about ourselves that potentially may result in negative evaluation from another person.

   d. is one where there is a power differential between those participating in the conversation.

   e. involves interdependent parties who are highly educated and identify differences of opinion about important topics.

4. The family life cycle stage that involves accepting emotional and financial responsibility for yourself is

   a. leaving home as a single young adult.

   b. getting married.

   c. preparing for retirement.

   d. living in retirement.

   e. making end-of-life decisions.

5. The family life cycle stage, characterized by launching children and moving on, involves the following second order changes in family status:

   a. Maintaining your own and/or couple functioning and interests in the face of physiological decline

   b. Dealing with the loss of a spouse/partner

   c. Developing adult-to-adult relationships between grown children and their parents

   d. Differentiation of self in relation to your family of origin

   e. Dependence on parental support

6. The three levels of agreement in the decision-making process are

   a. consensus, conflict resolution, and acceptance.

   b. consensus, accommodation, and *de facto*.

   c. cooperation, conflict resolution, and *de facto*.

   d. consensus, cooperation, and *de facto*.

   e. *de facto*, accommodation, and cooperation.

7. Which of the following is at the core of the financial communication process?

   a. Decision making

   b. Talking

    c. Self-checks of your perceptions

    d. Knowing your account balances

    e. Consensus building

8. The problem-solving loop is a guide for disclosure and decision making. Which of the following phases incorporates talking about alternatives and considering the pros and cons of them?

    a. Phase 1

    b. Phase 2

    c. Phase 3

    d. Phase 4

    e. Phase 5

9. When parents work, take care of their children, and provide for the economic needs of their family, they are performing which of the following family communication concepts?

    a. Self-disclosure

    b. Family dynamics

    c. Family stability

    d. Family roles

    e. Family rules

10. When children comply with the expectation that they should be ready for dinner at 6:00 p.m., they are demonstrating which of the following family communication concepts?

    a. Self-disclosure

    b. Family dynamics

    c. Family stability

    d. Family roles

    e. Family rules

Essay Questions

1. Define, describe, and provide examples of the problem-solving loop and its four phases. How does talk influence this model? How can this model guide your family's disclosure and decision making?

2. How do family roles and rules function in family day-to-day activities? Provide examples to illustrate your points.

3. Define self-disclosure. How does self-disclosure contribute to the process of discussing and making decisions about financial planning?

4. How can conflict assist families in discussing financial planning? Provide examples to illustrate your points.

5. Describe how the family life cycle stages model can help illustrate the many developmental changes that take place within one family. Specifically, select one life cycle stage that is particularly illuminating for your understanding of how families change over time.

2

MONEY BASICS AND ITS BAGGAGE

LEARNING OBJECTIVES

After reading this chapter, you will be able to do the following:

1. Describe how money can be viewed as a "problem" and as a "path" to financial goals

2. Describe the role of money and the emotional controversy it can create

3. Define a "need" and a "want" and the differences between them

4. Explain the role that communication plays in family financial planning

5. Identify the reasons why families are reluctant to discuss financial planning

CASE STUDY 2

Christmas Comes Early to the Jones Household: Part II

In chapter 1 you were introduced to the Jones family. As the parents of two young children, Dave and Sally Jones want to teach their children about careful spending. Dave and Sally's family backgrounds demonstrate a commitment to earning and saving money through hard work in order to attain goods and services. Participating in church and Sunday School activities are ways that Dave and Sally use their time and talents to benefit others rather than thinking only of themselves. They were in the midst of planning a family discussion to help their children make careful Christmas gift expenditures. Now, Dave and Sally want to talk with Max (age eight) and Audrey (age five) about "needs" and "wants." How can they approach the topic of Christmas giving with a discussion of needs and wants that will be consistent with their values? (Northwestern Mutual Life Insurance).

Sally and Dave need to select a convenient time and place for having a family meeting about needs and wants. Based on their children's ages, they set aside 30 to 40 minutes for the discussion. Sally and Dave need to agree on the strategies needed to fully cover this family financial topic.

Children often pattern spending habits from what they observe in their parents. What family life examples are there of necessary expenditures that represent needs? What types of expenses are wants that the family could delay or do without? Sally and Dave need to consider what would be clear, simple and age appropriate definitions of wants versus needs. Max as an eight-year-old may understand the need for heat, electricity, food and shelter but views wants as what makes him happy. Audrey at age five, trusts her parents to meet her daily needs unaware of expenses and may look to Max or TV commercials for guidance on wants.

Prior to having a discussion Sally and Dave could discuss recent family expenditures that can serve as illustrations of either a need or want to Max and Audrey. This list of categorical expenditures could serve as the starting off point about how money is used first to cover needs before buying wants. As noted at the end of chapter 1, Sally and Dave could use Internet research to make the discussion of wants and needs relevant and entertaining for Audrey and Max (Morin). Creating a list of family expenditures over the last year, Dave could ask Max and Audrey to guess whether each item could be classified as a want or need. Sally could explain why each expenditure is either a want or need after each guess. How a family spends money can be tied to their beliefs in how family resources are to be used for the greater good. Dave and Sally might also discuss how parents in their church have dealt with teaching children about wants and needs in relation to their belief system.

As part of the learning process, Sally and Dave need to use family buying opportunities as a means to illustrate differences between needs and wants. When going to the grocery store or mall with Max and Audrey they can have their children identify whether an item is a want or need as it goes into the shopping cart. Alternatively, they could ask Audrey or Max to identify three wants and three needs in the store. By turning their next buying excursion into a game, Sally and Dave will be able to reinforce the concept of needs versus wants while demonstrating that learning about finances can be a fun activity.

As a means of further reinforcing how money expenditures on wants and needs can impact families, Dave and Sally could have a family movie night and show a Christmas film that deals with how money is spent. Some possibilities might be *The Muppet Christmas Carol*, Dr. Seuss's *How the Grinch Stole Christmas, I Want a Dog for Christmas, Charlie Brown,* or *A Charlie Brown Christmas.* If time permits, they could also introduce the connection between payment for needs and wants within the family budget.

Learning the importance of funding needs first is important to the concept of budgeting later on. As a way of introducing this idea in a store setting Dave and Sally could give each child a small sum of money, say $5, to purchase two items. The idea is to have Max and Audrey make one purchase that is a need, and the other that is a want. After buying the two items, Max and Audrey can talk with their parents about their choices. Depending on the success of this activity, the discussion could continue to reach into the area of family values and budgeting.

Dave and Sally can emphasize the importance of providing for Max and Audrey's needs first with wants happening second. The implicit need for planning and self-control will probably arise during this discussion. When this does, Dave and Sally can refer to their family values of hard work and saving to reach their financial goals, whether the goal is in the form of a gift for someone, providing for a need, or saving to purchase a want. Self-control may be a challenging behavior because impulse products are so prevalent in stores. Talking about strategies to overcome the impulse to make a purchase, such as sticking to the grocery list, should be an ongoing discussion.

As you continue reading in chapter 2, think about additional strategies that any of the Jones family members might raise to discuss money, emotional ties to money, and the communication concepts that can help during the talk.

THE ROLE OF MONEY AND THE EMOTIONAL CONTROVERSY IT CAN CREATE

Money is often viewed as a problem. We hope to persuade you to begin thinking about money not as a problem, but as a path to achieve your family goal of financial stability and growth. Money is the means to an end when thought of as a path. A path is a road leading your family to a destination, however your family defines the destination. Communication is key to the dialogues we have within our original family. We learn money's function and necessity at an early age. Let's consider how our views of money and our emotional attachment to it are formed.

Views of money and family communication are likely to begin in childhood. As toddlers, we depend on our parents to provide shelter, food, and clothing without regard to how they are attained or the way these resources are allocated. At this early stage, it's difficult for children to differentiate between wants or needs.

A **need** is any purchase that is required in order to live a productive and useful life. A **want** is any item that a person can do without and still be able to survive. Often the issue of what is a necessity arises when parents go with children to the grocery store to buy food for the family.

After seeing items placed in the shopping cart, purchased, and brought home to make a meal, children learn that grocery stores are where food, a basic necessity, is provided. They also realize that their parents are exchanging money (cash, "plastic," or smart phone) to obtain these goods. However, what may be obscured is the difference between a need versus a want.

Children logically conclude that all items in a grocery cart are necessities because they are coming home to be consumed. There is no distinction between meat and produce, as opposed to packages of candy strategically placed in the checkout lane. If a child has experienced the pleasures of candy and a parent rolls up to the checkout counter, the chances are fairly good that the child will point out a missing necessity in the family shopping cart.

To a toddler all items in the grocery store are necessities; candy is close at hand, and therefore, candy needs to be in the family shopping cart. As a consequence, an all-too-common public discussion and negotiation will occur about the relative merits of candy as one of the basic food groups. In this moment, there is no one-size-fits-all method for explaining important financial planning distinctions between necessary food items that fall within the family budget and overall health and those that don't. A child's age, the cost and size of an unhealthy snack, previous discussions on the topic of healthy food choices, close proximity to mealtime, and urgency to complete the conversation/transaction without creating a scene may be significant variables in addressing this issue.

For children beyond the age of 3, who can understand reasons for choosing one action over another, a grocery conversation over candy can be a teachable moment, if approached within the parameters of family communication. Where this discussion takes place is important to having a productive exchange about wants versus needs, and why buying candy instead of fresh fruits, vegetables, protein, dairy, and produce items runs counter to the health and well-being of the family. If such an encounter occurs in the checkout line where others are waiting to pay for grocery items, the discussion will be brief and may lead to a demonstration of parental stress, frustration, and perhaps anger, with little likelihood of a desirable change in the child's behavior with future grocery visits, particularly if after all the fanfare the parent eventually buys candy in order to make a successful and hurried exit from the store.

Choosing the time, place, and setting for having a discussion about needs and wants are important ingredients for family members to reach common conclusions about this topic. Discussion of family financial issues should occur at home or in a quiet setting, where each member feels part of the conversation, with time sufficient to cover everyone's concerns. Exchanging ideas about food choices with children, on the way to the grocery store, at home while preparing a meal, or at the end of dinner when desserts are being served may allow opportunities to discuss what food items are necessary against those that are treats to be consumed less frequently.

Later, as children become older and can more fully reason about choices, discussing healthy food selection may lead to broader perspectives on wants and needs. Within this context, it may be possible to begin identifying and classifying family needs and wants. At this juncture, needs such as electricity, gas, water, sewage, heating, cooling, and home and auto maintenance can be introduced in the discussion. Once identified, these needs can also generate a discussion about cost and how these items are paid for in the family budget.

When discussing family financial planning with children, tone of voice and organization of the conversation are just as important as topics being covered. Young children may pick up facial cues and voice inflections more than what is being discussed at a family gathering. If parents are shouting, disagreeing with each other about key concepts, and/or appear angry, children may become confused or fearful about what is discussed. A distasteful feud that erupts about financial planning will not lead to further development of a process intended to bring members together to improve family finances.

Parents should exchange ideas on how best to bring up financial planning topics during family conferences and reach an agreement on how, in what place, and the manner in which discussion evolves. It would be helpful to decide who may best moderate the conversation and how the other partner can assist in explaining financial planning ideas. One goal should be to attain a family consensus that encourages everyone to work together on achieving financial planning goals. Discussions characterized by soft voices, nonjudgmental exchanges, and encouragement are more likely to help families embrace and utilize financial planning tools to better themselves. Now that we have considered the role of money in meeting our wants and needs, let's now consider the role of communication in family financial planning.

THE ROLE THAT COMMUNICATION PLAYS IN FAMILY FINANCIAL PLANNING

The **financial planning process** involves making and implementing plans to acquire and allocate funds to meet short, intermediate, and long-term financial goals. The steps to creating and executing this process are the same for individuals, couples, families, businesses, and nonprofit organizations. However, one major difference is the amount of work required to complete a financial plan when more than one individual is involved.

An individual who develops a financial plan does so by considering individual needs, resources, goals, and ability to execute action plans. A family seeking to create a financial plan must consider the needs, resources, goals, and abilities of all family members. Completing an individual financial plan rests with what one person is able to accomplish, while a family financial plan depends on every family member being in agreement and fully invested in the plan. As a consequence, it is unlikely that a family financial plan will be very successful if family members are unaware of the process and elements of the plan, due to a lack of communication.

Despite this critical element, some families begin the financial planning process by handing it over to one family member or an outside advisor. Certainly, this method of financial planning is better than nothing at all. However, if a family is to significantly benefit from financial planning, the process needs to be adopted and embraced by family members who will be carrying out the plan that has been mutually agreed upon.

Recent survey findings highlight the importance of financial planning, as well as the difficulties that arise when financial decision making occurs without communication. In the 2018 Planning and Progress Study conducted by Northwestern Mutual, 87 percent of respondents agreed that nothing made them happier or more confident than feeling like their finances were in order. However, 28 percent indicated that financial anxiety made them feel depressed at least once a month, 41 percent said that financial planning issues impacted their relationships with spouses/partners, 19 percent experienced financial disagreements with significant others, and 38 percent noted issues with family members other than partners/spouses over finances.

While communication may not be a panacea for resolving all family issues, it is unlikely problems can be addressed without everyone identifying and mutually agreeing on ways to overcome them. However, one of the greatest difficulties in obtaining communication on financial issues is getting the conversation started.

The Reasons Why Families Are Reluctant to Discuss Financial Planning

Let's consider six reasons people are nervous about money and financial planning.

1. A lack of background and understanding of finances

   One impediment to financial planning is that **finances**, funds that are available to meet specific needs, have not been taught as a lifelong skill in most high schools and colleges. As a consequence, few people have a familiarity and confidence in discussing finances. More recently some states have begun to mandate the teaching of financial literacy in high schools, which will help the next generation be more familiar with financial concepts. However, with this educational initiative there are still likely to be differences in financial knowledge within the family that inhibit those with less knowledge from entering the discussion of financial planning.

2. Concern about the amount of time required to do financial planning

   Family financial planning requires all members be engaged in the process. Organizing meetings, collecting information, leading discussions, developing next steps, completing financial planning tasks, and keeping everyone on track will take a commitment of time and energy from all family members. For some family members, it may be hard to see the benefits from such an activity, given the perceived time it takes to get everyone engaged in family financial planning.

3. Dependence on one family member to do the financial planning

Given the time and required commitment to develop a family financial plan, it's often easier to have one person create and implement such a plan. Families may rely on one member to do all the financial planning for reasons of simplicity and saving time. As a consequence, the one earning the most money may do the budgeting and decide where funds are spent. Over time, family members are likely to turn over more and more of the financial planning to one person as a comfortable way to have financial decisions made for them. Having one member do all the planning, however, creates a large time burden for them. It often leaves some family members unaware of what actions have been taken and why those actions were implemented.

4. Remembrance of past financial planning failures

Even though financial planning is a process that involves periodic review and updating, often financial planning is done on an ad hoc basis. A person may develop elements of a financial plan (e.g., prepare a budget or complete a financial balance sheet) when applying for a loan. A change in employment status may also elicit some financial planning, particularly with a job layoff. However, these one-time events may not lead to a desired goal of making good financial decisions on a long-term basis, and as a consequence can cause family members to view financial planning as a time-consuming, ineffective means of decision making.

5. The possibility of handing all financial planning tasks over to a financial advisor

Given the variability or lack of an understanding of financial planning by family members, some are likely to embrace the idea of having an outside, financial planning expert devise and institute the family financial plan. An outside financial planner may be viewed as an objective arbiter of family financial decision making, who has the knowledge and experience to navigate the thornier issues related to finances. A financial advisor may be unaware of the wishes and desires of all family members and is not likely to consult with each family member about the financial plan. Many financial plans are drawn up without input from children or young adults within a family. Often a family will change financial planners when an advisor moves to a new job or retires. In such cases, the family will need to select and educate a new advisor about their current plan and their financial planning goals.

6. Fear of having to deal with the results from financial planning

Many people put off financial planning for fear of finding out more about their financial position than they want to confront. Rather than identify and deal with finances, they would prefer to avoid making a financial plan that requires them to first assess their financial position. As a consequence, financial planning may be delayed or avoided for many years for fear of having to deal with the results of a financial assessment and plan. One major benefit to developing a financial plan is determining your financial position and then being able to address how you can improve it. Without a financial plan there is no understanding of current financial position.

As you reflect on the six reasons why people are reluctant to discuss finances, consider additional deterrents you have experienced or observed that make talking about money and financial planning difficult.

Connection between Finances and Communication

As we have begun dealing with money, finances, and communication, you have learned that communication can be an emotional, personal, and stressful activity. Family members are likely to have differing opinions about how money is acquired, earned, and spent over long periods of time.

Communication, or the lack of it, about money and personal financial decisions have far-reaching consequences for families. Communication about financial matters impacts family relationships now and in the future. The "m" word, *money*, elicits emotions that range from stress and anxiety to fulfillment and feelings of reward. Such strong reactions to the meaning of money come partly from our family history, experiences with money in our own families growing up, and personal encounters with money growing up. The way one's primary care givers, usually parents, dealt with money and financial decisions influence our perspectives of money today.

Most people think that financial communication begins between a committed couple. Yet, how each partner was raised to know about and discuss finances largely influences how well he or she will collectively communicate and make decisions in this area. If the two were given little direction about budgeting, saving, insurance needs, and retirement from their parents or caregivers, they may be at a loss to start a conversation about financial issues when they are married or in a committed relationship. How parents and caregivers raise and educate their children about finances has an effect on future relationships between themselves, siblings, and possible marriage or committed partners.

Even as a single person, communication within one's immediate family about finances can influence relationships between parents and siblings. For example, based on individual needs, parents may provide more financial assistance for one child over another. A child may require greater financial assistance to achieve an educational, business, or career goal. This difference in financial assistance may lead to misunderstandings, hurt feelings, and long-term resentment between and among family members, if the reasons for financial decisions are not openly discussed.

Often families avoid communication over financial issues that involve difficult choices. This lack of communication leaves family members to guess the reasons for the choices that may be far from the truth, shaded by personal perspectives on a financial matter. Not to communicate about finances is a decision that will impact family relationships, just as a decision to use the financial planning process can encourage families to identify, discuss, and make decisions about financial issues. Within this context the financial planning process is a tool to facilitate family communication about finances.

Most of the financial planning decisions faced by families are the result of the evolving life cycle stages of the family, which include such events as marriage or commitment, creation of a home, birth of children, provision for dependents, protection of the family, taking care of parents, and securing retirement funds and distributing wealth at the end of life. For example, what is important to us as young singles may change as we embark on marriage, living alone, a long-term committed relationship, a new career, or further education. Developmental changes, such as care giving for children or other adult family members, transitioning from work to retirement, or establishing permanent residence through the purchase of a home will require planning, budgeting, and, more importantly, discussion and decision making with those affected by the subsequent financial decisions while reaching these goals.

Both the financial communication and financial planning processes facilitate continuing communication, tenacity, and incremental steps toward reaching mutually agreed-on financial goals. The following chart serves to map the financial life cycles stages for a family and coincides with the family life cycle stages identified in chapter 1.

The stages of the family and financial life cycles (table 2.1) show how financial decisions are made as a family progresses and transitions from one life cycle stage to the next. During birth to adolescence, parents are responsible for meeting their children's basic needs, food, shelter, health-care, safety, and early education.

TABLE 2.1 The Stages of the Family and Financial Life Cycle

Family and financial life cycle stage	Financial planning transitions	Secondary financial transitions
Being born to adolescence	Meeting needs and understanding basic financial concepts	a. Providing food, shelter, safety, education, and health care by adults b. Introducing the financial concepts of needs, wants, allowance, savings, budget, and living within means
Leaving home: Single young adults	Accepting emotional and financial responsibility for self	a. Moving toward financial independence by obtaining first job, finding housing, and living within a budget b. Making major financial decisions about debt through purchases such as auto, insurance, education, and retirement plan
The joining of families through commitment, union, or marriage: The new couple	Commitment to new financial relationship with partner by making joint financial decisions and plans	a. Establishing income streams b. Dividing expenses c. Saving for joint financial goals d. Creating and maintaining an emergency fund
Families with young children	Accepting children into the financial planning system	a. Introducing to children the financial concepts of needs, wants, budgeting, and saving b. Modeling the financial concepts c. Encouraging small jobs, chores, and allowance d. Setting up educational funds e. Establishing retirement and insurance plans for life, health, and disability f. Creating wills and trusts
Families with adolescents	Increasing flexibility of family financial boundaries to permit children to become adept at making purposeful financial decisions	a. Encouraging adolescents to seek and negotiate outside jobs b. Helping adolescents save to achieve small and intermediate financial goals c. Seeking adolescent input on some major financial decisions such as auto, vacations, and home improvements

(continued)

TABLE 2.1 The Stages of the Family and Financial Life Cycle (*Cont.*)

Family and financial life cycle stage	Financial planning transitions	Secondary financial transitions
Launching children and moving on	Changing roles as financial advisors for single or married children	a. Determining the specific type and amount, if any, of financial help to adult children b. Revising, if needed, financial priorities of retirement and estate planning c. Planning for grandparents' care
Families in later life	Accepting shifting financial goals	a. Revising and planning for retirement b. Deciding when to retire c. Identifying activities and activities that can be afforded in retirement d. Shifting to new retirement income and expenses e. Creating medical directives and durable power of attorney documents f. Reviewing and updating wills and trusts; asset liquidation; tax and estate plan; executor or trustee selection; and final arrangements and expenses
Death	Life ends	a. Completing final arrangements and their payment b. Filing death certificate c. Filing final tax return d. Distributing life insurance proceeds, financial assets, and property

Adapted from McGoldrick, M., Garcia Preto, N.A., & Carter, B.A. (2016) *The Expanding Family Life Cycle: Individual, Family, and Social Perspectives* (5th ed.) New York: Pearson and Gitman, L. J., Joehnk, M. D., & Billingsley, R. S. (2014) *Personal Financial Planning* (13th ed.) : South-Western Cengage Learning.

As children become more aware of their own desires, the topics of needs and wants are introduced when buying household items and navigating gift giving. Parents with young children will need to obtain sufficient life insurance and a will as part of their financial planning. Though unexpected catastrophic consequences should a parent die prematurely are hard to think about, a plan nevertheless needs to be in place.

In the middle and high school years, adolescents are introduced to the financial concepts of budgeting, saving, earning money from small jobs, an allowance, and setting and achieving reasonable financial goals. In this stage, adolescents can and probably should participate in their family's financial planning discussions. By increasing their involvement, adolescents can strengthen their understanding and commitment to financial decisions made as a family. For example, teenagers may have an interest, and some amount of expertise, in various preferable features when buying the family car. They may prefer a vehicle that has the body, sound system, and speed that conveys smart, classy, sporty transportation, as opposed to one "old people" might drive. The elements of cost, financing, durability, maintenance expenses, insurance, and resale value may not be the important features they are thinking about when considering the next family car. Yet, by including teenagers in this financial decision, they will become more aware of the financial investment in the purchase. When parents listen to their teen's concerns about the type of car, they communicate to their teen that their opinion counts in the family decision. Additionally, the parents are providing a valuable framework for their teens to use when making a future car purchase on their own.

You might be thinking that the communication and financial planning transitions for the stages birth to adolescence and families with young children are similar. You are correct! When growing up, children and adolescents become acquainted with communication and financial planning transitions through their parents. As adults, these learned financial planning practices are likely modeled for their own children, if they have them.

When launched for their original family, young adults move toward financial independence. This process may have begun during high school. Frequently, parents assist their teenager with purchasing a car, evaluating career choices, and examining the cost of education. Once the now adult children leave home and enter a committed relationship, the parental relationship changes to one of supporting the union and serving as financial advisors upon request. Later on, if the committed couple has children, a new set of financial transitions will occur as they support their offspring, in ways similar to what their parents did for them.

Parents with young children will address the financial need to have sufficient life insurance and a will to handle planned and unexpected life events. Even if a young married couple has very little in the way of financial assets to distribute at death, it is important to prepare a will as soon as children enter the family. A will establishes who will become guardians for children if both parents die in an untimely event such as a car, plane, or train accident.

Parents, after launching their children, will transition to their own financial focus by fully funding a retirement plan. During this stage, the now empty nest couple will make tentative decisions about when, where, and what activities to pursue during retirement. An estate plan needs to be developed also.

Once the couple enters retirement, the financial planning process evolves into budgeting income from their assets to meet their living expenses. Retirement planning involves deciding when to take Medicare, Social Security, and pension and individual retirement account (IRA) benefits, making decisions about health care coverage, whether to live in the home where their children were raised or sell the house and relocate, evaluating tax issues related to retirement, and identifying enjoyable, meaningful activities to pursue in retirement are all part of this stage.

By the time a retiree reaches age 70.5, financial decisions about end-of-life issues we hope will have been discussed with family members. This conversation should occur earlier depending on family history related to the onset of dementia, Parkinson's disease, or other illnesses that could impact health care decision making. Since adult children are likely to be the ones carrying out the desires expressed in a medical directive or hold power of attorney, the family financial communication process will return to its original roots. The adult children will become caregivers, counselors, and financial advisors to their parents.

A bumper sticker recently made the rounds that offered a unique perspective, "Be kind to your children, they may decide where you will receive nursing care!" To some extent, the time and effort parents make in communicating and working with their children on financial matters while growing up serves as the training ground for end-of-life decision making. In some cases, adult children make great sacrifices to help parents in the last years of life. Adult children become caregivers who monitor the activities and medical assistance given to an ailing parent. Generally, adult children living closest to their parents will share more responsibilities. These responsibilities may involve a commitment of time, and in some cases lost income if the need arises for them to give up employment to care for their elderly parent. Avoiding discussing long-term care giving and fairly recognizing the services provided by a family member can result in misunderstandings, misgivings, and disagreements upon the death of a parent.[1]

---

[1]   Two anecdotal cases serve to illustrate this end-of-life financial issue. One of the authors observed the following instances of discord related to caregiving. In the first, the youngest son, with two other siblings, left a musical career in New York to attend to his mother in the Midwest. In recognition of his assistance, the mother paid him monthly income for care. These monthly payments were a fraction of what the costs would have

Then, why is it so difficult for families to communicate about money? Many people think communication about finances occurs once there is a relationship established between a committed couple. In many cases, the beginning of a long-term relationship will trigger communication about money matters. For example, even the issue of whether a date is paid for by one or both partners, as opposed to collectively splitting expenses, carries implications about individual views of money and who controls the purse strings. How each person learned about needs and wants, setting up a budget, saving money, purchasing insurance, funding retirement, and buying a home, either from their parents or through formal education, will influence their ability to discuss these matters. If such conversations or lessons did not happen, they may be at a loss to start a conversation about financial issues for their relationship and household.

The age of the couple when children may arrive is yet another factor in how children learn about money. For example, if parents have children late in life, it is likely that the children may be unaware of the financial decisions in terms of saving, investing, and budgeting that took place prior to their birth or while they were infants. The standard of living that these children enjoy may be far different than those children who may have been born to younger parents.

Additionally, if one partner has more knowledge in a financial area, the tendency may be to offload all decisions on this partner rather than discuss a financial issue and come to a mutually agreed decision. Over time such an arrangement can encourage financial decision making in all areas of the household being made by one partner without the knowledge and consent of the other. Lacking an understanding of basic financial terms

---

been for her to be in a nursing home, a place she wished to avoid until needing hospice care. These payments were never discussed between family members. However, upon the mother's death, the two other children contested the payments, sought to have them used to reduce the younger son's inheritance, and were successful. The dutiful son did not want to risk being alienated from his siblings by contesting this issue. Another similar case involved a younger daughter who lived in the family home to take care of her mother. Dementia set in and the mother had to go into full-time nursing care. The mother and daughter had agreed that in that event the daughter would stay in the family home and monitor the nursing care. However, this understanding was not in writing and when the mother died, the siblings sought to have this daughter's inheritance reduced to reflect the benefit she received by staying in the family home. Both cases highlight the need to discuss end-of-life care with children at a time when a parent's wishes can be expressed and documented to avoid problems after death.

and communication strategies may inhibit or limit conversations about money and finances. Further, as long as the financial decisions appear compatible with the silent partner in the financial decision making there is a good chance no communication will occur. However, if a financial decision should turn sour, a conversation may take place where the silent partner finds fault and financial planning is a source of conflict rather than harmony. This book is intended to encourage and promote active discussion of financial planning issues by all participants within a family or long-term relationship.

Often families avoid communication over financial issues that involve difficult choices. Lack of communication leaves family members to guess the reasons for choices, which may be far from the truth and shaded by personal perspectives on financial matters. Avoiding communication about finances is a decision that impacts family relationships by leaving open questions surrounding why or how financial decisions were made. In some instances, a parent may make a decision on behalf of a child that may not be wanted or desirable. For example, if a parent were to allocate money in an education fund that requires the child attend a specific college or university, the child may not appreciate the gift if he or she prefers to go to a different school.[2]

On the other hand, a decision to use financial planning to stimulate family discussion is a conscious effort to open family dialogues about finances. The financial planning process is designed to promote communication that encourages open, empathic, and creative conversations to solve problems and achieve common financial goals.

Unfortunately, many families spend a great deal of time and effort avoiding communication about financial planning issues. Even though divorce rates have declined in last two decades, currently, about 42 percent of all marriages of those age 46 or less ended in divorce (U.S. Bureau of Labor Statistics). Financial distress caused by the lack of money or high amounts of debt has been identified as a significant cause of divorce (Dew et al., 615). Ironically, it is at the end of these marriages that the financial planning process begins. A divorce will require the couple to

---

2   State-sponsored, prepaid 529 funds allow parents to save for their children's college education by buying investment units that defray the cost of attending college at one of the state public universities. In some cases, the value of these accounts to the parents and their child depends on that child going to a state university. If not, the amount saved may be refunded but at less value than what it would be if the child attended a state school. See Statler, Kate.

exchange views on financial resources, asset values, and their claims over family assets.

Another area where people avoid discussing financial planning issues is at the end of life. Over the years, a number of high-profile individuals, such as Prince, Aretha Franklin, Martin Luther King, Jr., Abraham Lincoln (who was a lawyer), Howard Hughes, Jimi Hendrix, Kurt Cobain, Steve McNair, or Pablo Picasso died intestate, without a will. In these cases, probate courts assume that the deceased individuals, having had every opportunity to declare their wishes and failing to do so, were indifferent with respect to the distribution of their assets. These estates generally pay higher probate taxes and will have whatever is left distributed equally among heirs.

Why would someone who has spent so much time and effort amassing a fortune allow a disinterested court judge to distribute his or her wealth? A major reason lies in the inability to communicate one's desires about his or her possessions. The fear of death, thinking there will be some time later to write a will, a lack of understanding of financial planning concepts related to wills and estates, as well as the inability to communicate with family members about last wishes, all contribute to the phenomena of dying without a will. The 2005 case in Florida involving Terri Schiavo's wishes relating to life support is another example where family communication in the area of financial planning would have been helpful. Lacking a medical directive, a lengthy court battle ensued among Schiavo family members over what would have been Terri's wishes in being left in a vegetative state (Caplan). The financial planning process oftentimes leads family members to consider executing such documents as a power of attorney, living will, and medical directive to explicitly state their wishes concerning medical treatment should they become incapacitated and unable to make their own decisions in the future.

The financial planning process is a tool for opening up communication that evolves from the family and financial life cycle stages presented in table 2.1. Chapter 3 will provide an overview of the six steps to the financial planning process with elaboration and illustrations on the first three stages of this process: preparing a family financial mission statement; developing short-term, intermediate, and long-term financial goals; and preparing a family financial statement analysis.

CHAPTER SUMMARY

In chapter 2 you were introduced to how money can be viewed as a problem and as a path to financial goals; the role of money and the emotional controversy it can create; the concepts of needs and wants and the differences between them; the role that communication plays in family financial planning; the reasons why families are reluctant to discuss financial planning; and the preliminary overview of the stages of the family and financial life cycle.

SELF-CHECK QUESTIONS

True/False

1. The financial planning process involves making and implementing plans to acquire and allocate funds to meet short, intermediate and long-term financial goals.

2. A family seeking to create a financial plan must consider the needs, resources, goals and abilities of adult family members rather than children who don't make decisions.

3. In a recent Northwestern mutual planning and progress study, 87 percent of respondents agreed that nothing made them happier or more confident than feeling like their finances were in order, while 41 percent said that financial planning issues impacted their relationships with spouses/partners.

4. While communication may not be a panacea for resolving all family issues, it is likely problems can be addressed without everyone identifying and mutually agreeing on ways to overcome them.

5. One reason why a family can easily discuss financial planning issues is because most children are taught financial concepts at an early age.

6. One impediment to family financial planning is the perceived time it takes to get all family members engaged in the planning process.

7. Some family members may not become engaged in the financial planning process when it is delegated to one family member who makes all financial decisions.

8. A "need" is any item that a person can do without and still be able to survive.

9. Discussion of family financial issues should occur at home or in a quiet setting, where each member feels part of the conversation, with time sufficient to cover everyone's concerns.

10. Views of money and family communication are likely to begin in childhood.

Multiple-Choice Questions

1. Which of the following research findings suggest why families are reluctant to discuss finances?

    a. A lack of background and understanding of finances

    b. Concern about the amount of time required to do financial planning

    c. Dependence on one family member to do the financial planning

    d. Fear of having to deal with the results from financial planning

    e. All of the above

2. When are our views of money likely to begin?

    a. During childhood

    b. During teenage years

    c. During early adult years

    d. When we start working

    e. Our views of money fluctuate throughout our lives

3. Which of the following family expenditures would be considered a need?

    a. Buying tickets to an NFL game for family members to attend

    b. Purchasing a vacation package to stay on Maui for Christmas

    c. Paying the utility bill to heat the family home

    d. Paying for a new Rolex watch

    e. Buying a 70-inch HDTV on Amazon

4. When discussing financial planning issues with children it is important to
    a. wait until they are seniors in high school when they have experience buying things.
    b. wait until they have a job and can spend their own money.
    c. wait until you have a disagreement with them over money to allow everyone to fully invest in the conversation.
    d. have a discussion at home, in a quiet place where all family members can participate in the conversation.
    e. b and c

5. A need is
    a. any purchase that is required in order to live a productive and useful life.
    b. any purchase that may be needed to live a productive and useful life.
    c. any expenditure that a needy person would like to have.
    d. a short-term expense that can be paid for on a credit card.
    e. a long-term expense that needs to be paid with a debit card.

6. Remembering past financial planning failures often is the cause for
    a. families to delegate financial planning activities to one family member.
    b. families to see the need to develop a financial plan and stick to it.
    c. families to avoid doing financial planning.
    d. families to avoid credit card debt.
    e. families to go on spending sprees because financial planning doesn't matter.

7. One significant reason why families avoid financial planning is

   a. it costs too much money to implement.

   b. family members are afraid to learn about their financial position and confront what to do about it.

   c. it might result in too much savings and the need to learn about investing.

   d. it leads to conversations where family members are able to offer perspectives on finances.

   e. it might lead to a better understanding of wants versus needs for the family.

8. A family seeking to create a financial plan must

   a. consider the needs, resources, goals, and abilities of all family members.

   b. hire an outside financial planner to make financial decisions on behalf of the family.

   c. appoint the family member who makes the most money to make all the financial planning decisions.

   d. avoid preparing financial statements because they may be too depressing.

   e. have one or two family members take a financial planning course so they can make all financial decisions for the family.

9. A want is illustrated in which of the following examples?

   a. Buying gas to drive to work

   b. Purchasing a diamond necklace

   c. Acquiring a new video game

   d. All of the above

   e. b and c

10. One of the problems with having one family member do all the financial planning is

   a. that family member may enjoy doing the work and won't feel burdened by the time commitment.

   b. some family members may be unaware of financial planning decisions made on their behalf.

   c. that family member is not being compensated for all the work that he or she is doing.

   d. the family would like to have more money to spend on wants, but the one doing the financial planning isn't interested in spending money.

   e. the family member would have to go back to the university to complete a degree in financial planning to be truly helpful.

Essay Questions

1. Describe how communication can help your family move from thinking of money as a problem to money as a path for accomplishing financial goals.

2. Describe how money elicits an emotional attachment. What factors contribute to our emotional ties with money? How do these factors develop and influence us throughout our life cycle stages?

3. Identify the six reasons why families are reluctant to discuss and engage in financial planning. Describe each reason in detail and offer an example to illustrate your point.

4. Identify two of the communication process strategies that can be used to discuss financial issues, such as needs and wants with young children. Provide an example of how you might introduce the topic of purposefully spending money.

5. Discuss the role that communication plays in family financial planning and why it is important in promoting stability within the family.

SECTION 2

THE NITTY GRITTY OF FINANCIAL PLANNING

3

GETTING STARTED
DEVELOPING AND TALKING THROUGH A FAMILY FINANCIAL MISSION STATEMENT

LEARNING OBJECTIVES

After reading this chapter, you will be able to do the following:

1. Describe the financial planning process

2. Explain what a family financial mission statement entails

3. Describe and develop the short-term, intermediate, and long-term financial goals for a couple or family

---

CASE STUDY 3
Love, Marriage, and Defining What Is Important

Karen Sanders and Tim Turnbull are avid runners who met on the track during their senior year in college. After several fun runs (5 miles you can walk or run) and two marathons (21 miles you endure), they fell in love and decided to get married. Karen grew up in a family with three siblings: two older sisters and a younger brother in Eden Prairie, Minnesota. Karen's mother teaches high school math, and her father works in marketing for General Mills. Karen was interested in math and science at an early age and decided to go the biochemistry, pre-med route in college. Her parents were able to save up enough money to assist with her undergraduate education, and that help, along with academic scholarships, enabled her to graduate with only about $10,000 in student loan debt.

Tim grew up with one older sister in the small farming community of Spring Valley, Minnesota. His father farms 300 acres of land that produces corn, wheat, and soybeans. Tim helps his father wherever he can and has been doing so since middle school. Tim's stay-at-home mother has been responsible for taking care of him and his sister while his father works the fields. Tim became interested in computers in high school, and as a consequence, he will be graduating with a degree in computer science. With support from his parents, along with money saved in high school and college, scholarships, and income from paid internships, Tim will graduate with only $5,000 in student loan debt. Tim has a computer job lined up with a Fortune 100 company at an initial annual salary of $45,000 in the Twin Cities as a result of completing two internships during his junior and senior years of college. However, once Tim graduates, he will need to start paying on his student loan. Tim hopes to pursue an MBA in the future after spending time working in computer science.

Recently, Karen and Tim received some exciting news. Karen has been accepted into the University of Minnesota Medical School in Minneapolis. The cost of medical school for in-state students is about $65,000 a year including books, tuition, and room and board (University of Minnesota). Karen's student loan debt will not come due as long as she remains in graduate school pursuing her medical degree. Their wedding is planned for June. Tim and Karen are discussing how they can work together to determine their financial goals that will sustain and strengthen their marriage. Their plan is to (a) create a list of shared values that they will use to develop a family mission statement; (b) determine short, intermediate, and long-term goals that reinforce the family mission statement; and (c) describe how their shared values, the mission statement, and financial goal setting will enhance their conversations about financial decisions. Tim and Karen are particularly aware that they are in the "new couple" stage of the family and financial life cycle. How will knowing the primary and secondary financial planning transitions of this stage be helpful for them in developing their mission statement to address the medical school education cost for Karen? As you read chapter 3, consider the concepts introduced in chapters 1 and 2 to help you assess Tim and Karen's financial situation and planning.

Chapter 1 introduced communication, the concepts that are a part of it, and how these concepts apply to family communication. The nature of communication, self-disclosure, conflict, family roles, family rules, and the family life cycle stages were defined and described. The family problem-solving loop for discussion guidance and the stages of the family life cycle were presented. The parallel financial stages of the family life cycle were introduced in chapter 2, along with the challenges for talking about money and financial planning for families. All of these concepts are important to reinforcing that financial communication within the family involves discussion requiring self-disclosure and decision making.

As we stated in chapter 1, we value talk. The ability for couples and families to address and discuss the topic of finances and financial planning is why we are writing this book. Though perhaps imperfect in practice, the financial communication process is imperative to frame the financial planning process that will be more fully developed in this chapter.

As you read chapter 3, consider how you would advise Tim and Karen in developing a mission statement and financial goals as part of their financial planning process. Based on what you have learned, reflect on how Tim and Karen might go about discovering their values and using them to build a couple's family mission statement.

In this chapter you will learn how to help Tim and Karen identify how they can use their mission statement to define short-term, intermediate and long-term financial goals. As the mission statement is developed, their agreed-on short-term, intermediate, and long-term financial goals will require discussion and decision making. You will need to help them identify ways that they can have conversations about their shared values that will influence their financial goals. Finally, the advice that you give them may require them to revise their mission statement now and in the future.

THE FINANCIAL PLANNING PROCESS AS A MEANS TO BETTER COMMUNICATION WITHIN THE FAMILY

Financial planning is a process that incorporates communication to help families make money decisions based on information rather than emotion. The process requires family members to lay out their values and mission, determine goals, set priorities, and develop methods for meeting those objectives. Doing so enables the family to make a realistic appraisal of their financial position, execute financial action plans, and commit to a periodic updating of the financial plan. The communication concepts of discussion, self-disclosure, the family problem-solving loop, and decision making drive the process. The financial planning process encourages the expression of views regarding future goals and the priorities and methods of what is attainable within a set period of time.

The financial planning process consists of the following six steps:

1. Talking about money and its uses within a family, identifying the values a family has, and developing a family financial mission statement from these conversations

2. Determining short-term, intermediate, and long-term financial goals for a family

3. Identifying, through financial statement analysis (budgets, income statements, and net worth determination), the current family financial position

4. Using information from steps 1 through 3, creating a plan to achieve the family mission and financial goals

5. Periodically evaluating how well the family mission and financial goals are being met

6. Re-evaluating the family mission statement and financial goals and updating the financial plan

The six steps to the financial planning process allow a family to define what they value, determine reasonable goals, create action plans for meeting these objectives, monitor their progress, and revise their plan as conditions change. To further understand how the financial planning process may be incorporated into financial communication and decision making, we will begin describing the purpose and function of steps 1 and 2.

STEP 1: DEVELOPING A FAMILY FINANCIAL MISSION STATEMENT

So, what is a family mission statement and why is this important to financial planning? How do families begin to talk about the process when there might be some differences of opinion?

Establishing how acquiring, earning, spending, and investing money are to be viewed within the family will determine the way a financial plan is developed. Some families may view money as a means to an end.

Earning, saving, and investing funds to reach a goal is what makes money important to them. Others may see money as an end in itself. Their focus is on accumulating as much wealth as possible and money is the yardstick for measuring success. In most cases families find themselves somewhere in between. Money is used to meet a set of financial goals, and the more money they have, the greater the number of goals that can be met.

The financial planning process begins with the definition of **family values**. For our purposes, the business definition of values highlights the relationships that connect families and financial decision making (Business Dictionary).

Values are important and are lasting beliefs or ideals shared by the members of a culture about what is good or bad and desirable or undesirable. Values have major influence on a person's behavior and attitude and serve as broad guidelines in all situations. Some common business values are fairness, innovation, and community involvement.

Step 1 should include a discussion and resolution of such issues as the following:

- What earned income may be used for individual versus family needs?
- Who decides how money is to be spent?
- How will disagreements about money be resolved?
- Should there be provision for individual family members having their own personal assets?
- What are the ground rules for discussing and making decisions about the uses of money?

Family Financial Mission Statement

The **family financial mission** statement is a statement that outlines the values, aspirations, and guiding principles of a family that informs how financial goals and decisions will be made. The initial step toward creating and defining the family financial mission statement begins with identifying the shared, common values embraced by individual family members. Few people ever write down what values are most dear to them. How can this be, when we are living in the information age, where access to personal opinions are readily available on Twitter, Facebook, or LinkedIn?

One explanation may be that your values reveal an intimate part of who you are, which entails a high level of self-disclosure or risk in being negatively evaluated. Another possibility is that if someone has never been challenged to write a mission statement, he or she may not have felt the need to discover the values he or she lives by. It may have been acceptable to occasionally be aware of certain values when making a decision, but not have the urge to write them down. So, why should people spend time identifying their values and coordinating them to form a mission statement?

There are several reasons why value setting and writing a mission statement are beneficial to the financial planning process. First, when making a financial decision it is important to have a basis for measuring the advantages and disadvantages of a particular choice. A mission statement that outlines core family values can serve as a yardstick for measuring whether a particular financial decision either reinforces or detracts from a family's values.

Second, financial decisions should be consistently made to support a family's value orientation. If a family has not written down what values it's operating under, there are likely to be inconsistencies in the way financial decisions are made with respect to a family's values. A family that buys a home in a low-crime neighborhood but drives an older car needing brake repairs may not see any discrepancy in terms of safety. Yet, if the family has a mission statement that gives safety and security as a top priority, they are less likely to miss the importance of giving immediate attention to repairing brakes on the family car.

Finally, a mission statement will encourage family members to review, reaffirm, change, and commit to the values that are important to them. A mission statement is a living document that requires periodic updating to reflect the ever-changing conditions faced by the family. An outside, unexpected event, such as the Great Recession of 2008, during which the gross national product fell, unemployment was high at 10 percent, and home values fell by approximately 30 percent, is likely to cause a family to reassess what is important to them in terms of values, money, relationships, and commitments. Having a set of core values that are highlighted in the family mission statement provides an effective framework for reconsidering and reestablishing the values family members hold dear.

Several methods exist for finding a set of mutual family values. One strategy for developing a set of values is to have family members write down their own life values and share them at a family meeting. This list of values could then be used to create a set of common family values. The sample list of values in Table 3.1, while not comprehensive, may serve to help families think about those values that are important to them.

TABLE 3.1 Sample List of Values Embraced by Individuals and Organizations (Clear, 2019)

Empathy	Humility	Faithfulness	Honesty	Authenticity	Fairness
Helpful	Friendly	Courteous	Service	Trustworthiness	Supportive
Love	Kindness	Loyal	Poise	Work Ethic	Compassionate
Knowledge	Respect	Steadfastness	Peace	Security	Safe
Obedient	Thrifty	Ethical	Reverence	Brave	Self-respect
Responsible	Learning	Happiness	Persistence	Competency	Determination
Creativity	Balance	Achievement	Maturity	Acceptance	Forgiveness
Purpose	Usefulness	Affirming	Purposeful	Giving	Hope
Excellence	Godly	Commitment	Faith	Hard work	Recognition
Stewardship	Accomplishment	Accountability	Mastery	Satisfaction	Generous
Openness	Family	Togetherness	Employed	Teamwork	

A second method is to have each family member answer the following questions that may identify moments when their values are evident (Mind Tools):

- When did you feel happiest? What were you doing? Why were you so happy?
- When did you feel proud of yourself? What were you doing and why were you so proud?
- When did you feel fulfilled and satisfied with yourself? What were you doing and why were you satisfied and fulfilled?

Answers to these questions can help detect the set of values a family may want to use when developing a mission statement.

A third approach to discovering values is to first find the values that are most important and then begin associating other values to it. For example, if security is a significant value, you could ask the following:

- What makes you feel secure? The answer might be, I feel secure when I am employed.
- What makes you feel secure when you are employed? When I am recognized for my accomplishments.

Using this method can help you uncover a hierarchy of values from security to employment, followed by recognition and accomplishment. As part of this values search process you could select another important value, such as affirmation. You could construct the following questions:

- When do you feel affirmed? I am affirmed when accepted by others.

- How are you accepted by others? When they respect and show kindness toward me.

The answers to these questions establish a link between affirmation and the values of acceptance, respect, and kindness. By using one or all of these techniques, a family can create a list of values most important to them and then move toward the process of constructing a mission statement.

The stage of the family and financial life cycle, where constructing a mission statement will occur, will depend on when a family begins the financial planning process. Ideally, an awareness of financial planning has been a part of a person's formative years. If not, there is no better place to start than today. If a newly married couple, such as Tim and Karen, are starting to write their mission statement, they are currently in "the joining of families through commitment, union, or marriage stage." In this stage the couple makes a commitment to a new financial relationship with each other by making joint financial decisions and plans. As adults, they are discussing and making decisions. Other stages of the family and financial life cycle, such as "families with young children," will presumably rely on the parents to be responsible for developing a rank order of family values.

Over time and the adapting stages of the family and financial life cycle, the role of children will be important to the discussion of shared values. "Families with adolescents" will most often have input from older children and teenagers. Whatever stage the family is currently experiencing, in the beginning stages of mission statement development, parents could create a list of values that they developed in their marriage and share them with their children. The children could then add to the list and ask questions about why their parents included certain values. A family will need to prioritize their values before drawing up a mission statement.

An overall family mission statement provides the purpose and reason for the family's existence. The mission statement provides the focus for all family decisions. It offers a perspective on the main priorities of the family within the financial planning process. For example, if the mission statement includes language relating to adequate provision for the educational needs of all family members, then the development of an educational fund would have to be considered a financial goal.

Mission statements can vary in length. They can consist of a paragraph or go on for several pages. However, in order for all family members to be working toward the same set of goals, everyone needs to participate in mission statement development, understand the statement, and be willing to invest time and effort in achieving its ideals. The mission statement will likely change over time as the family adapts to changes, accomplishments, and challenges. A young couple might develop a mission statement along the following lines:

Example 1:

Our family will be based on a loving, caring relationship between and among all family members based on the common spiritual values of self-sacrifice, forgiveness, and service to others. We respect the individual needs and contributions of each family member. In addition, we will strive toward applying the golden rule, honesty, humility, and goodwill in dealing with family members and those outside the family. The family will seek to preserve itself by maintaining the physical and financial health of all members.

Family financial resources will be shared to promote the physical and educational needs of family members, with health and welfare having top priority within this context. Parents will mutually determine family financial goals and the health and welfare of children until age 18. After age 18, children will participate in decision making related to these issues.

Education will be an important priority for children, with parents making every effort to provide financial assistance in ways that will lead each child to reach his or her full potential for leading a productive life and contributing to society. Every effort will be made to resolve family financial disputes through discussion and compromise within the family. However, should there be a major disagreement that cannot be resolved, family members will seek to obtain a solution through the help of an outside family and/or financial counselor.

Every two years, this mission statement is to be reviewed by the family with a discussion and determination of whether and how it may be updated. If conditions change and the need arises, the family will meet and consider ways to update the mission statement and financial plan immediately.

Example 2:

> As a committed couple we will maintain a respectful relationship where we will daily feel honored and cherished. We value navigating life together by sharing experiences, domestic responsibilities, and making joint decisions to the degree that we can. We will strive to live a healthy lifestyle and meet the needs for our minds, bodies, and spirits.
>
> If we are blessed with children, we will honor and cherish them by providing for their physical, spiritual, and mental well-being through modeling a loving home and educating and training them to become creative and contributing members of our Earth. We will discuss family concerns by regularly sharing meals, activities, and interests.
>
> Our mission statement will be reviewed every year or sooner if a need arises.

Mission statements begin by outlining the most important values and then adding values that support those of higher priority. If the mission statement begins with "We support the inherent worth of every family member," later on it might include the values that support this position. For example, additional values might include statements such as, "We will promote a healthy lifestyle and medical care for members," or "We support educational and training opportunities for our children."

The family mission statement is an agreement laying out the values, aspirations, and life perspectives that guide family decisions toward selecting and reaching specific financial goals. With a set of prioritized values, a family can write a mission statement that clearly outlines family standards for establishing financial goals and decisions. Two additional sample family mission statements are provided, highlighting the general format of a mission statement.

1. Introduction of core values and family purpose: The statement begins with language that highlights the purpose and aspirations of the family: "Our family aspires to be known by our commitment to (two or three top-ranked values) in our relationship to ourselves and others." Alternatively, the mission statement could start with, "The [Family Name] family's purpose is to demonstrate (two or three significant values or principles) to ourselves and those we meet."

2. Statement of values and principles that reinforce core values and family purpose: After the introductory sentence outlining the purpose, the next sentences would include values and principles that

connect and reinforce that purpose. These declarations could begin with, "Our family will meet its purpose by (principles, values and actions that support primary, core values)." Alternatively, you could write, "The [Family Name] holds that these shared values and principles are essential to defining who we are and what we stand for: (principles, values and actions that support the family's purpose)."

3. Role of the family: Following this language is a component that defines the role of the family. These statements highlight how family members will communicate, support, nurture, direct, connect, and sustain each other.

4. Wealth perspectives, uses and responsibilities: After outlining the role of the family, it is important to define the family position on wealth. Wealth includes not only money, but the talents, educational abilities, training, and experiences of family members. This section focuses on how wealth will be used to support family values and principles. It will highlight perspectives on what wealth means in relation to the family's purpose and role to promote its shared values and principles.

5. Resolving family differences over values, principles, wealth and finances: The last module addresses how the family will go about resolving future disagreements among members in regard to values, principles, and financial matters.

Family Mission Statement
Example 1: The Jones Family

Our family wants to be known by our commitment, faithfulness, and hard work to ourselves and those we meet.

Our family will meet its purpose by loving each other and living lives of hope and forgiveness.

Our family roles are to communicate respectfully with one another. Not only will we speak respectfully to each other, but we will give each other a full hearing when we need to be heard and to listen without distraction in return.

Our family will support each other by providing physical and emotional safety in the form of a safe home and the emotional reassurance that we are loved and respected.

Our family will nurture each other by giving and receiving love, lifting one another up, and encouraging each other daily in our words and actions.

Our family will be led by our parents as they are the adults who guide and have the responsibility to care for their children and the larger entire family.

Our family will connect with each other at a minimum of one mealtime daily. During mealtime no devices will be present. We will have conversation and discussion about our daily activities, what we might have learned, and one good experience that we had.

Our family will sustain each other by spending time together in family activities, such as walking after dinner, playing golf, camping, fishing, and other outdoor activities. As a family of faith, we will sustain each other through prayer, supporting fellowship and counting the many blessings we have.

Among the blessings that we enjoy are the abilities to work, earn wages and salaries, and accumulate and manage wealth. Our family views money as a means to an end to provide the needs that we must have to live. Our home, clothing, food, education, and necessities such as insurance, transportation, and health care are fundamentally important to our well-being. Beyond meeting the needs of our family, money will be saved for emergency funds, educational pursuits, savings and retirement accounts, and recreation. As a family we like to travel and spend time together. Accumulating funds for these pursuits are sought after our family's basic needs are met. Our family is also committed to giving to others through tithes and offerings at church and to charitable donations that we have agreed, as a family, to support.

As a family, when conflicts and disputes arise over the values, principles, and financial directives , we will have discussions to clarify the specific conflict point or disagreement. Since our family values define who we are, we will seek alternatives, compromise, or collaboration to find ways where the point of conflict or disagreement can be resolved.

This family mission statement will be reviewed every year to revisit and reinforce the values and principles by which we will interact with and live together. If a family member would like to review the mission statement sooner than this, a family meeting will be called to discuss the need for review.

Family Mission Statement
Example 2: The Smith Family

The Smith family's purpose is to demonstrate acceptance and achievement to ourselves and those we meet.

The Smith family holds that these shared values and principles are essential to defining who we are and what we stand for by responsible hard work and teamwork as a family and being compassionate to others.

The roles of our family include communicating, supporting, nurturing, directing, connecting, and sustaining each other. We will do this by the following:

1. Communicating: Our family will have a family meeting every two weeks on a Sunday evening to discuss our past activities, successes and challenges, and upcoming schedules for the following two weeks. We view ourselves as a team that needs regular interaction to "coach each other up." If Sunday evening cannot accommodate everyone's schedules, we will find an alternative day that same week. Our family aspires to have regular, thoughtful, and respectful communication with each other. It's great to be a Smith!

2. Supporting: Our family will support each other in the decisions that we make. Although we may not always agree, we will support each other in the individual decisions that we make. When conflict arises, we will talk with each other rather than avoid the topic to try to resolve the point of disagreement. As a family that views itself as compassionate, we will strive to relate to each other in this way as well as those outside our family.

3. Nurturing: Our family will be emotionally available to each other. While this is an ideal that may have challenges in meeting, our goal is to encourage the talents, gifts, and interests of one another. Knowing what each of us is doing in our lives is of significant importance. Our shared financial goals, education, and family activities are the most important ways that our family can nurture each other. Family members will work together to support the needs of each member, recognizing that each of us have different talents, needs, aspirations, and challenges.

4. Directing: Our family will encourage and support the direction where our parents guide us. As a couple, our parents will communicate with

each other to establish shared goals for the family. For the children, they will look up to and defer to the parents' decisions in the goal setting. Questions will be allowed to be asked from both the parents and the children.

5. Connecting: Our family will connect not only with and for itself, but we will connect and participate in the community in which we live. Volunteering, participating, and making donations to our family's selected charities are part of our team-based identity.

6. Sustaining: Our family views itself as a compassionate team for encouraging goal attainment and developing our individual abilities and group achievements. We will sustain these values and principles until such time that the family seeks to focus on alternative values and principles. We sustain these aspirations by communicating, supporting, nurturing, directing, and connecting in the ways that have been stated.

The Smith family views money and wealth as strong financial connections to and with each other. Our family seeks to be debt free and to save and accumulate wealth for long-term life events, such as a large home, camping vacations, and educational goals. Practicing the habit of meeting our needs versus our wants is our path to achieving these financial goals.

In the event that, as time passes, individual family members differ in this attitude about money and wealth accumulation, the family member may raise questions and ideas in the regularly scheduled family meeting for discussion, consideration, and potential decision making. The family mission statement will be reviewed annually and can be adapted sooner if the majority of the family wishes to do so.

Reading sample mission statements from individuals and organizations can offer valuable insights into the structure and way values, principles, and actions can be interwoven to produce a clear, comprehensive statement of mission (See, for example, Bresciani; Vanguard). Organizations such as universities and colleges produce mission statements designed to call attention to their values, and they serve as a guide for faculty and administrators making decisions. Referring to your school's website and mission statement will help you see how it was constructed as well as the specific values and principles that guide your institution.

Sample family mission statements are available on the Internet. Pinterest, faith-based organizations, and home-schooling groups are just a few places where mission statements are posted. While considerable information exists on the Internet relating to financial mission statements, ultimately, it's the family that prepares a document best representing its purpose, values, principles, and perspectives on wealth. If the mission statement is to be a useful and helpful financial planning tool, it has to be one that members embrace and that members agree represents their interests.

Once the mission statement has been developed, it should be shared and discussed with all family members. Even though children may not be writing the first mission statement, at some point as they grow older, they should have input into its further development and feel part of the process. As a mission statement gets periodically evaluated and updated, having children participate in creating draft revisions is helpful to their understanding of the first step in the financial planning process and how they can develop one of their own when leaving home.

As the family evolves over time, this mission statement will need to be updated and revised. For instance, once the last child completes his or her education and training, finds employment, and begins living away from the home, the mission statement will need to reflect these changes to the family. The focus of the mission statement may emphasize meeting the physical and health needs of the parents, leaving off the funding of educational needs. Later, the education focus may be reinstated in the mission statement should grandparents decide to provide for the education needs of their grandchildren.

The development of a family mission statement is as varied as families are. What all should have in common, though, is the need for everyone to first agree on the values that define who they are to themselves and others as a family. An additional element to the family mission statement can be how the family and its members want to be remembered.

How often should you change your mission statement? In general, the mission statement should be reviewed periodically, at least once every two years. If a major change occurs within the family, such as medical emergency, completion of educational goals, receipt of an inheritance, change of job, or job-related move, then the mission statement should be revisited immediately.

Identification of the problem: The mission statement "problem" is to create a document that incorporates all family members' opinions about what is most important to them as a family. Using one or both of the activities listed will help generate what the family finds most good and desirable in opposition to what the family views as bad and undesirable. From these lists, the family can discuss the items and why they are included on the respective lists. As the discussion ensues, stating how the lists will move the family toward the writing of the mission statement may need to be repeated, sometimes several times.

Conflict or differences of opinion may arise during the discussion, depending on the stage of the family life cycle. For instance, if a 15-year-old adolescent participates in the discussion, the teenager may be unclear whether a 4-year college degree is a personal goal. This opinion may be in direct opposition for one or both parents. If agreement is not met, then the "value" of education could be restated as a formalized plan for the teenager to pursue post high school graduation, whether it is a two-year, four-year, or trade apprenticeship. The point is to keep the educational "value" in the mix so that it will remain in the mission statement with a specific goal to be determined.

Restatement or formulation of goal: Emphasizing that the family financial mission statement is an ongoing and flexible document reinforces that life's ebb and flow as well as personal growth and change of point of view can be revisited at a later time. The point of the family financial mission statement activity is to create an understanding of the family values, in general. This general understanding recognizes that the communication process and the financial planning process are close partners in the family financial planning process. Perfection is not required. Active participation in the process is the way to collaborative decision making.

Sometimes discussion gets stuck or sidetracked. When this happens, it's okay to restate the purpose of the activity as a means to reach the objective of writing a mission statement. Creating a family financial mission statement may take more than one session. Remember that you are not in competition with anyone to meet the goal. Several family meetings can give everyone a chance to think about and reflect on the discussion. In a perfect world the time to reflect may help everyone see and understand positions that differ from their own. The point is to plan on conflict happening at some point and not be afraid of it. Plan for it. You have communication strategies now to help the process. There's benefit in the activity of talking together about the importance of money as a reflection of your family's values. Greater awareness makes the self-disclosure less intimidating as your family navigates the subsequent steps in the financial planning process.

The next section, step 2, moves the mission statement along to goal setting.

STEP 2: DETERMINE SHORT-TERM, INTERMEDIATE, AND LONG-TERM FINANCIAL GOALS FOR THE FAMILY

Once a mission statement has been put to paper, it can be used to identify financial planning goals that reflect the values found in the family mission. Goals can be defined in terms of short-term, intermediate, and long-range time frames.

General characteristics of family goals are the following:

1. Financially measurable

2. Specific in terms of time and amount needed to fulfill the goal

3. Realistically attainable in an allotted period of time

Not all goals can be financially measured. In Example 2, it is difficult to financially measure feeling honored and cherished on a daily basis. Yet, sharing the domestic responsibilities and providing for a healthy lifestyle through mind, body, and spirit implies that certain purchases will need to occur for these values to be realized. How these purchases and services will be obtained becomes a financially measurable endeavor. For example, a healthy lifestyle may involve eating organic foods, paying for alternative health services, and participating in spiritual retreats. These goods and services all cost money and so are financially measurable and require planning to meet these goals.

The time needed to fulfill the goal is significant to the financial process. When determining your short-term, intermediate, and long-term financial goals it's important to be cautious about the length of time needed to accomplish your objectives. If you classify a long-term goal as a short-term or intermediate goal, it may to lead to decisions that impair financial health. For example, if you announced that you intended to be a millionaire in the next year the steps taken to achieve such a feat might involve taking substantial financial risk. Some people faced with such a goal might gamble hard-earned money on speculative ventures with possible high returns, but more likely result in the loss of invested funds. It is better to be prudent in setting your goals within a reasonable time frame, especially one where you are likely to achieve success and not risk the loss of funds. Pursuing an unrealistic goal can jeopardize financial stability by introducing greater risk of losing money while trying to achieve a long-term objective in a short period of time.

Just as with dieting, one can always ambitiously announce that he or she intends to reach a goal in a short period of time. "I plan to lose 50 pounds in the next two weeks!" Medically speaking, even if such a goal were to be realized, the steps necessary to reach it might not be healthy.

Goal attainment must be realistic for the time period. Sometimes we are overly optimistic in what we can accomplish in a day, week, month, or year. Striving to meet the objective in the time we think that we should or would like to is just not possible. So, be kind to yourself in designating a time period for meeting a goal. Just as the previous example illustrated, desiring to lose 50 pounds in two weeks may be a wish, but it will take a longer period of time to lose the 50 pounds in a healthy way. So too, if the desire is to save for a down payment on a home, pay off your college debt, and start investing in a savings plan, consider the unexpected events in life that may dissuade or discourage the achievement of the big financial goals. In other words, don't be afraid to make a number of long-term goals when you really would prefer them to be short-term or intermediate goals.

Short-Term, Intermediate, and Long-Term Goals

Short-term goals represent those financial objectives that can be achieved in a year or less. Developing a budget, keeping expenses at least 20 percent less than the couple's or the family's total income, making annual contributions to an IRA account, or saving $1,000 each year for the down payment on a home are examples of short-term objectives.

Intermediate goals are those items that can be accomplished within the span of one to five years. Objectives such as having enough down payment money to a major purchase, such as a home; setting aside enough money in an emergency savings fund to cover 6 months of salary; or accumulating $10,000 in an IRA retirement account are intermediate goals.

Long-term goals are those objectives that would take more than five years to complete. Some long-term goals include saving money to assist children with their college education, which may take 15 to 18 years to accomplish, and fully funding your retirement at age 65, which might take 30 to 35 years to achieve.

Financial goals should reflect the values presented in the mission statement, demonstrating family priorities and objectives. If the mission statement outlines the primary importance of food, shelter, and providing educational opportunities for family members, then there should be financial goals that align with these value characteristics. Conversely, if there are financial goals that are outside the scope of the mission statement, then either the mission statement needs to be revised or those goals need to be eliminated in favor of the ones that support the family mission.

The process for creating a set of short-term, intermediate, and long-term financial goals begins with family members developing a list of future goals. The idea is to initially prepare a long inventory of goals that fit within the family mission statement. For example, if the mission statement says that the health and well-being of family members is a priority, then a short-term goal might be researching, evaluating, and buying health insurance to adequately cover family medical expenses. A second short-term goal might include buying dental, drug, and eye care plans to cover family members. Finally, a third short-term goal would be to buy locally grown produce or raise your own food to ensure fresh nutritional quality for the meals the family prepares.

Short-term goals may be intermediate and long-term goals as well. Adequately funding health insurance, medical expenses, and dental, drug, and eyecare coverage spans all time periods for families. Family well-being would also encompass having sufficient funds to cover expenses in an emergency. An emergency might be the loss of a job, car accident, destruction of the family residence due to fire, flooding, tornado, hurricane, or any other large loss event. As a consequence, a short-term goal would be to research, investigate, and purchase auto, homeowner's and flood insurance, as well as begin saving money toward an emergency fund to replace salary income for six months.

All of these tasks associated with financial goal setting can become overwhelming. You might be thinking that this is all too much and abandon the whole process. Don't despair. The exhaustive list that is being compiled will be narrowed down into a more manageable set of goals. This part of the financial process is the "heavy lifting" that helps put family members' thoughts on paper. It will get better after this activity.

After the extensive list of goals has been written, the next step is to see if the goal can be measured in financial or money terms. If so, then the goal can be classified as a *short-term*, *intermediate*, or *long-term* objective. The following chart illustrates how goals can be categorized and organized.

Family Financial Planning Goals

Short-term goals: Goals that can financially be achieved within 1 year or less:

- Complete a budget for next year and use it to track and regulate living expenses
- Begin funding an emergency fund
- Take advantage of employer's retirement plan, if available
- Start to pay off student loan debt, if this applies to your situation
- Pay credit card balances, if possible, when due to avoid penalties and interest charges. If this is not possible, be sure to pay by the due date and try to pay more than the minimum required payment
- Research factors to consider when buying a home

Intermediate-term goals: Goals that can be financially met in one to five years:

- Invest funds in an emergency account that can draw some interest; the higher the interest, the better
- If an employer's retirement plan is available, consult with a human resource staff member to set up the maximum return on these funds
- Develop a strategy that will reduce by half any student loan debt, if applicable
- Create a home down payment fund for first-time buyer(s)
- Begin saving for college education or other fund for post–high school children use
- Begin saving in a Roth IRA for retirement

Long-term goals: Goals that will require more than five years to financially achieve:

- Accumulate the equivalent of 6 months' earnings in an emergency account to cover six months' worth of expenses in the event of a job loss or other family emergency
- Completely pay off student loan debt in 10 years, if applicable
- Purchase an affordable home with desirable location and amenities
- Accumulate, through savings and investment, a college education fund, or its equivalent, that can pay half of each child's four-year college education at a public university
- Fully fund retirement by age 65

The listing of financial goals involves several steps. First, a determination is made as to whether the goal involves a financial decision. The goal of being happy, while commendable, cannot be financially measurable. However, goals related to shelter, food, and education are financially measurable and may offer some level of happiness.

Second, each financial goal should be related to a value found in the family mission statement. If the mission statement values the health and safety of family members, then the financial goal of finding suitable housing is appropriate in reinforcing those values.

Third, within each category, short-term, intermediate, and long-term goals, the set of goals is prioritized, with those listed first having highest priority. For example, in our illustration, the first short-term goal is preparing a budget and so it would be developed before proceeding down the list of other goals. Part of this goal-setting process allows everyone to see how short-term, intermediate, and long-term goals are interconnected. If you have a short-term goal to begin paying off student loan debt, it is connected to the intermediate goal of reducing that debt in half within five years.

Ultimately, the short-term and intermediate goals lead to meeting the longer-term objective of completely paying down student loan debt. Over time, long-term goals become intermediate and then short-term goals. Initially you have a goal of fully funding retirement by age 65; accomplishing this feat will be the result of setting aside and investing funds on an intermediate and short-term basis. Hopefully, when you are 60, five years away from retirement there will no longer be that long-term financial goal of funding retirement because it will then be an intermediate goal. At age 64, that intermediate goal becomes a short-term goal.

Some short-term goals may never leave the financial planning process. The goal of preparing a budget each year is a short-term objective that needs to be completed each year to maintain a family's financial stability. One benefit from having a history with permanent short-term goals is that they can become second nature and with experience can be completed more easily than when first initiated.

The Role That Financial Planning Plays in the Financial Communication Process

The financial planning process is a six-step tool for helping families communicate about money. It offers structure for (a) defining the family's values and mission; (b) choosing short-term, intermediate, and long-term financial goals, (c) determining the family's current financial position, (d) identifying financial action plans to enhance decision making, (e) evaluating the effectiveness of action plans, and (f) analyzing and updating the financial plan to improve the overall financial planning process. This chapter covers the first two steps that are the foundation for the financial planning. These initial steps outline how the family views money within the context of its mission statement and identifies the financial goals that reinforce these values.

Each step in the financial planning process builds on itself to permit family discussion on ways to address financial issues consistent with its values. A mission statement guides the types of financial goals a family will discuss and agree to.

CHAPTER SUMMARY

Chapter 3 introduced the financial planning process, the family financial mission statement, and the short-term, intermediate, and long-term financial goals for a couple or family. The communication processes of self-disclosure, the family problem-solving loop, and conflict were illustrators for managing the discussion and decision making that occurs during the financial planning process.

SAMPLE RESPONSE TO CASE STUDY 3:
Love, Marriage, and Defining What Is Important

By developing a set of shared values, Tim and Karen can discover what matters most to them in their marriage. How a couple spends money directly relates to their values system. Equally important is that how a couple spends money is important in sustaining their marriage. The family values instilled in Tim and Karen by their parents will inform where their values come from and which ones were most important when growing up.

Their respective parents' values can be a starting point for having a conversation about values they have at the start of their marriage. Another opener for beginning a conversation of this nature is to have Tim and Karen write down their values on separate sheets of paper and share the results with each other. They might select values that are important to them from the list of values found in this chapter. They could then identify those values common on both lists and discuss how they should be ranked on a comprehensive list of family values.

After creating this rank listing, Karen and Tim could then consider those values not common on their original lists to see whether some should be listed and ranked. Completion of a ranked list of family values can then be used to write a family mission statement with higher-ranked values introduced at the beginning of the document.

SELF-CHECK QUESTIONS

True/False

1. One possible explanation of why people never write down those values most dear to them is that values reveal an intimate part of who they are, which entails a high level of self-disclosure.

2. The family mission statement is an agreement laying out the values, aspirations, and life perspectives that guide family decisions toward selecting and reaching specific financial goals.

3. Financial decisions do not have to be consistently made to support a family's value orientation; what matters is whether there is enough money to reach family goals.

4. One strategy for developing a set of values would be to have family members write down their own life values and share them at a family meeting.

5. When thinking about money and its uses within the family, there should be a discussion about what earned income may be used for individual as opposed to family needs.

6. The financial objective to completely pay off all student loans in 20 years is an example of a long-term goal.

7. Completing a budget for this year and using it to track and regulate expenses is an example of a short-term goal.

8. Each financial goal should be realistic and measurable, but it doesn't have to relate to any of the values found in a family mission statement.

9. Some short-term goals, such as funding adequate health care, may also be considered intermediate and long-term goals.

10. The goal of being happy is a short-term objective that can be financially measured in a financial plan.

Multiple-Choice Questions

1. The reason(s) for taking the time to write down values and use them to develop a mission statement is (are)

   a. when making a financial decision it is important to have a basis for measuring the advantages and disadvantages of a particular choice.

   b. financial decisions should be consistently made to support a family's value orientation.

   c. a mission statement will encourage family members to review, reaffirm, change, and commit to the values that are important to them.

   d. all of the above.

   e. only (a) and (b).

2. A family mission statement

  a. outlines core family values that can serve as a yardstick for measuring whether a particular financial decision either reinforces or detracts from a family's values.

  b. is a permanent document that should never be updated because it represents unchanging family values.

  c. is developed from the short-term, intermediate, and long-term financial goals of every family member.

  d. can be created without developing a set of family values because it lays out aspirational guidelines that are merely suggestions.

  e. has nothing to do with the way a family allocates its financial resources.

3. The following is (are) values embraced by individuals and/or organizations:

  a. Honesty, trustworthiness

  b. Love, forgiveness

  c. Compassion, authenticity

  d. All of the above

  e. Only a and c

4. Key elements in the general format for a mission statement is (are)

  a. introduction of core values and family purpose.

  b. statement of values and principles that reinforce core values, family purpose, and role of the family.

  c. wealth perspectives: uses and responsibilities and ways to resolve family differences over wealth and finances.

  d. all of the above.

  e. only a and b.

5. A family discussion about how disagreements about money will be resolved is which of the following?

    a. Will never occur because the topic is too distasteful and unpleasant

    b. Will occur when discussing family financial goals

    c. May only be discussed by parents in private when children are not present

    d. Occurs in the first step of the financial planning process when a family thinks about money and its uses within the family

    e. Occurs when the family begins to develop a budget because that's when there can be a lot of disagreements about how money is to be spent.

6. Step 1 of the financial planning process should include a discussion and resolution of such issues as

    a. the ground rules for discussing and making decisions about the uses of money.

    b. who decides how money is to be spent.

    c. if there should be provision for individual family members having their own personal assets.

    d. all of the above.

    e. only a and b.

7. Part of the financial planning process involves

    a. a periodic review and updating of the family mission statement.

    b. applying for a new car loan.

    c. discussing who will be developing the household financial plan on his or her own.

    d. having a conversation on the amount of household debt the family can have.

    e. buying a new car to facilitate the family transportation needs.

8. Creating and accumulating a down payment fund that can be used for the first-time purchase of a home is

   a. an example of an unrealistic financial goal.

   b. a short-term goal that can become an intermediate or long-term goal depending on the time needed to fully fund the down payment.

   c. not financially measurable because it's too difficult to know how much you need in a down payment without knowing how much house you are going to buy.

   d. a goal best met by playing the lottery.

   e. not necessary because most banks will give you a home loan without requiring anything in the way of a down payment.

9. Saving up enough money for a child, now age 5, to pay half of his or her college education in the future is

   a. a short-term financial goal.

   b. an intermediate financial goal.

   c. a long-term financial goal.

   d. an unnecessary goal because the child will become a football star and get an athletic scholarship.

   e. not a financial goal because the cost of a college education 13 years into the future cannot be accurately measured.

10. One benefit from having a history with permanent short-term goals is

   a. they allow you to focus on current financial issues to the exclusion of longer, more distant objectives.

   b. they can become second nature and, with experience, be completed more easily than when first initiated.

   c. they allow you to introduce short cuts, such as eliminating the need to do budgeting.

   d. they can become intermediate goals.

   e. after a while you can ignore them in favor of pursuing intermediate or longer-term financial objectives.

Essay Questions

1. Describe the financial planning process and explain how it may help facilitate better family communication about money.

2. Explain how to go about developing a mission statement and how family values are incorporated into it.

3. Discuss the six steps to financial planning and tell how the first two may be used to define the values and financial goals of the family.

4. What are the three essential characteristics of a financial goal and how do they guide family discussions about goal setting?

5. Explain how short-term, intermediate, and long-term financial goals are interconnected in terms of a family meeting their financial objectives. Give an example of how a long-term goal may be related to an intermediate and/or short-term goal.

4

THE HARD PART
WORKING THROUGH A FAMILY FINANCIAL STATEMENT ANALYSIS

LEARNING OBJECTIVES

After reading this chapter, you will be able to do the following:

1. Define a family financial statement analysis

2. Describe how a budget is a plan for how money received will be spent

3. Explain how an income statement tells how money was made and spent

4. Describe how a balance sheet shows how well decisions were made about the budget

5. Identify and describe the financial position

CASE STUDY 4

Getting a Picture of Our Finances

Bill and Melinda Parks have been married for three years and have a son, Jimmy, age two. Currently they are renting a home for $1,300 a month, including utilities, in a suburb of Houston, Texas. Their monthly take-home pay after taxes is $6,500. Food, insurance, gas, telephone, Internet, and cable expenses average $745 a month. Miscellaneous expenditures for vacations, clothes, dining out, and football tickets amount to $500 per month.

Recently, Melinda read an article on September 15, about the steps to getting a home mortgage and found that financial institutions want to know a family's net worth when making a loan. The higher a family's net worth, the greater the chances a bank or credit union will approve them for a mortgage that helps finance the home they want. Bill and Melinda completed their family mission statement and identified their short-term, intermediate, and long-term financial goals as a result of these activities. One of their intermediate goals is to own a home in the next five years.

Based on the advice of the article that Melinda read, they have decided to calculate their current net worth position. After their net worth is calculated, they want to strategize how they might increase it each year. Bill and Melinda have identified the following financial items representing what they either own or owe others. They would like your help developing a balance sheet to determine their net worth and strategies that could increase that amount.

Savings at their credit union	$5,000
Checking account balance at their bank	$7,000
Credit card balance	$5,000
Current value of 2012 Toyota Camry (47,000 miles)	$12,000
Estimated value of jewelry	$1,500
Student loan debt [Bill: $20,000; Melinda: $5,000]	$25,000
Retirement accounts [Bill: $5,000, Melinda: $8,000]	$13,000
Furniture, clothes, housewares, owned and insured	$2,500
Certificate of deposit	$10,000
Current loan balance on auto loan	$5,500

As you read chapter 4, think about how Bill and Melinda will calculate their net worth. Identify the communication strategies that they can use to discuss and decide how to increase their net worth to meet their intermediate goal of purchasing a home in the next five years. Let's begin by taking up the financial statements and analysis.

THE FINANCIAL STATEMENT ANALYSIS

The financial statement analysis is a uniform, consistent, and objective method for assessing a family's short-term, intermediate, and long-term financial goals. The financial statement analysis is a two-step process. First, the analysis involves identifying and recording financial information that assesses how well the family is keeping expenses within the level of the family's income. Second, the analysis shows how what the family owns is growing in relation to what is owed to others. The financial statement analysis involves several documents: the **budget** and **income statements,** and a **balance sheet**.

The **budget** and **income statements** are short-term financial documents that allow families to discuss and decide what expenditures will be made in relation to their household income. A **balance sheet** is a longer-term financial document that shows what the family owns, called "**assets**," and are in relation to the family debt, called "**liabilities**," that is owed to others.

A **budget** is sometimes referred to as a *proforma* **income statement,** because it is a forward-thinking document that lays out what a family intends to spend in relation to the income that it expects to receive. A budget can be prepared for varying periods of time. Some families may develop a budget for the next month, three months (quarterly), six months (semi-annually) or a whole year (annually). Whether you do a budget every month or 3, 6, or 12 months is not as important as making a budget and sticking to it. Herein is where the communication strategies that we have been discussing since chapter 1 will help you in this financial process. We will revisit the concepts of self-disclosure, conflict management, and the family life cycle stages later.

Changing a budget after it has been implemented is not unusual. In some cases, additional income might come from extra work, a year-end bonus, tax refund, or any other unexpected income source. The additional income will create an increase in income over what was budgeted. The family will need to decide where these additional funds should be used to provide the greatest benefit for their family financial goals. These discussion and decision-making processes should include referring to the short-term, intermediate, and long-term financial goals that arose from the family values activity. As needed, your family should refer to these documents. Placing them in a high traffic area of your home, such as posted on the refrigerator or other often-used space, will frequently remind family members of the values, ideals, and financial goals that have been agreed on through your family discussion and decision making.

In other circumstances, expenses may increase from what was planned. Maybe utilities were higher this month due to lower temperatures and increased energy expenses. The car may require a repair that was not anticipated this month. These additional expenses will mean that the family must adjust the budget to find ways to pay for the unexpected expenses. In some cases, funds may come from savings created to meet unexpected expenses, such as money placed into an emergency savings fund.

The process of budgeting helps families see the larger picture of funding needs that may go missing without the benefit of planning. For example, when buying a car, some family members may look at the sticker price along with the trade-in value of the current car to determine whether they can afford their purchase. Other expenses such as the cost of maintenance, license fees, insurance, and money set aside for emergency repairs are items that need to be considered when buying a car. At the time of the purchase, a family should include within their budget funding allocations for all of these expense needs.

An **income statement** is a record of how money has actually been spent from the income received for a particular period of time. An income statement has reporting frequencies that mirror those of a budget, namely one month, three months (quarterly), six months (semi-annually) or a year (annually). However, in contrast to a budget that represents what *may* happen in the future, an income statement gives what *really occurred* in terms of family income and its expenses.

An income statement helps families evaluate how well they are allocating funds to meet their financial goals. A budget statement is aspirational; it shows how the family funds will be directed within a particular time frame to achieve financial objectives. The income statement shows how well these intentions are being met along with what adjustments are needed to increase the likelihood that the family's financial goals can be reached.

One of the common features for both a budget and income statement is their distinction between discretionary, as opposed to nondiscretionary, expenses. A **discretionary expenditure** is the payment for a good or service that can be classified as a *want*. It is something that you can do without but wish to have at the time of purchase. A **nondiscretionary expenditure** represents a good or service that is necessary to maintain the family. These expenditures are *needs*. Utilities, transportation, health and property insurance, taxes, food, shelter, and clothing are necessities that cannot be ignored in maintaining a family. Nondiscretionary expenses are of great importance when developing a budget or evaluating an income statement because they represent costs that cannot easily be left unfunded. You can't simply decide not to pay your taxes this year without incurring significant consequences. Such consequences are expensive penalties, interest costs, and substantial time filing a delayed return.

While the two choices, discretionary versus nondiscretionary expenses, may appear to be categorical in nature, there are some choices family members will need to make when trying to organize their expenditures.

For example, having a car for transportation may be viewed as a necessity; in other words, the car is a *need*. The lack of public transit to get to and from a job or go to school may require having a car to earn a living or secure an education. Under such circumstances, the family may decide to buy, maintain, and service an automobile.

This necessary and nondiscretionary family expense involves the type and cost of the car. Is a new $100,000 Tesla automobile a necessity or a luxury car purchase? Could the family possibly survive with a five-year-old Lexus RX 350 for $13,500 with 80,000 miles on it?

After the car is purchased, a set of nondiscretionary expenses will follow. Sales tax, license fees, auto insurance, maintenance, and upkeep costs are additional nondiscretionary expenses. With the Tesla purchase, the family will incur substantial, nondiscretionary expenses with insurance, taxes, and repairs on a $100,000 car. The lower-priced used Lexus offers transportation similar to the Tesla without all the high nondiscretionary expenses found with a more expensive car. Such distinctions need to be worked out during the family discussion and decision making about the type of car and budget for fulfilling the needed transportation requirements.

The Lexus or the Tesla will provide the transportation means to meet the needs of getting to a job or school. The style and accompanying expenses of transportation are highly variable given the car selected.

Another important consideration when making a discretionary purchase is to decide if you are creating a nondiscretionary expense. Anyone who has "negotiated" a cellphone, cable, or TV subscription agreement can readily understand how an initial discretionary purchase can blossom into an expensive two-year monthly fee and a nondiscretionary obligation to the family budget. As a consequence, when faced with a discretionary purchase that entails a long period of nondiscretionary payments (e.g., one year or longer), it makes sense to have family members thoroughly investigate alternatives.

Possible alternatives include

- getting the same level of service or product at a reduced total cost;
- doing without the discretionary purchase until the purchase is more attractive; or
- finding a lower cost alternative that may be similar to the one under consideration.

For example, in the last case, if the family is considering a one-year streaming video service such as NetFlix to access its movie vault, a virtually free alternative is to use the local public library. The library alternative requires taking the time to go to the library and selecting an older movie DVD to check out. Yet, the abundance of classic films may offer better entertainment than the large content offerings provided by a streaming media provider that has to be paid for.

Relevant questions to ask are the following:

- How much will you use a subscription each month to justify the required payment you make for the luxury of downloading content?
- How much is your time worth in seeking the entertainment at the public library that you would like to view that is cost free?
- Is a DVD rental service, such as Red box, a viable alternative to view an occasional new release that supplements the use of the public library?

Family discussions about alternative ways of obtaining goods and services, whether they be discretionary or nondiscretionary, ultimately leads to a better understanding of costs, benefits, and the most attractive way to address a financial purchase decision. Discussing how the seemingly small decisions influence the larger family financial goals will help your family regularly see the goals in action.

Building the Budget and Income Statements

A budget or income statement begins with a title that states the period over which income and expenses are to be considered. For a budget, the title might be **"Jackson Family Budget from April 1st to June 30th 20__."** For an income statement, the title might look like **"Jackson Family Income Statement for the Period of April 1st to June 30th 20__."**

The sequence of events in forming these financial documents relates to how they are used together. First, the Jackson family will prepare a budget from April through June. Then, at the end of each month, beginning in April, the Jackson family can prepare a monthly income statement, followed by a 3-month income statement from April 1 to June 30. The Jackson family will develop an income statement based on what actual income and expenses were made for each month from April 1 to June 30.

Family budget discussions to create the **"Jackson Family Budget from April 1st to June 30th, 20__"** will focus on estimating the likely income and expenses for the three months. When the three-month period is over, the family will develop an income statement of actual income and expenses.

You might be wondering, "Why do we have to prepare two separate documents that seem redundant?" The budget is anticipatory for your financial picture; the income statement is descriptive of what actually happened financially during the 3-month period. Both documents are helpful in the communication process of discussion and decision making. Looking at both the expectation (wishful thinking of a family budget) and the reality (in some cases harsh reality) of what happened can help a family clarify its values and shifting importance of goods, services, income, and expenses.

Family conversations can focus on how well the actual income matched with expenses. By looking at areas where actual expenses exceed those in the budget, discussions can address what may have led to these results. Was the original budgeted expense amount too optimistic in terms of using an unrealistically low expense figure? Did an unexpected emergency, such as car repairs, lead to higher than budgeted expenses?

By examining actual costs with what was budgeted, a family can improve how it budgets in the future. Additionally, family members can review the discretionary expenditures that may have led to higher-than-anticipated expenditures. Were expenses on travel, entertainment, or clothing higher than what was budgeted? How close was the anticipated budget to the reality of what really was reflected in the income statement?

Communication Processes Needed

At this point, with all of the questions, it's time to go back to the family problem-solving loop presented in chapter 1. The family problem-solving loop begins with the "identification of the problem." With the budget and financial income statement in hand, it's time to consider step 2, "restatement or formulation of the goal." How did the budget help the family anticipate income and expenses? Does the income statement for the same time period reflect this anticipation accurately? Does an adjustment need to happen? The "goal" of step 2 will probably remain the same because the "goal" reflects the family mission statement as well as the short-term, intermediate, and long-term financial goals of the family. The budget and the financial income statements will help the family to see potential patterns of income and expenses. If, over time, the family realizes that the amount of income falls short of its expenses, then moving to step 3, "assessment of resources" can focus discussions on ways to increase income or decrease expenses. For instance, taking on a part-time job, if time allows, or having a garage sale to sell unused, outgrown, or redundant belongings can generate income.

Alternatively, as stated, the family can assess whether to discontinue a service or entertainment for a short period of time. For example, in Ruth Soukup's book, *31 Days of Living Well, Spending Zero*, she challenges families to drastically reduce a family's grocery bill for 1 month by taking inventory of the pantry and freezer, using what you have on hand for meal planning, and purchasing perishable items like milk, eggs, and bread. This radical approach to limiting spending for 1 month sensitizes family members to the expense of buying food that stays in the refrigerator and spoils, fast food, take out, and restaurant meals. According to the U.S. Environmental Protection Agency, more than 38 million tons of food waste was generated by American households, most of which went into landfills. Focusing for a limited time, as a family, on the shared goal of reducing excess food purchases can energize and heighten awareness of how money is spent on nonessential food expenditures.

Does the family really need to stop at the local ice cream shop for a treat when there is ice cream in the freezer at home? Is the last-minute stop at a fast-food eatery really necessary after a long day? Was the coffee from the drive through really necessary to treat yourself? The tracking of behaviors can assist the family in accomplishing step 4, "generation of alternatives" to reduce expenses. Soukup suggests that weekly reflections will help the family see the challenges and rewards of creative meal planning, having a meal plan, and the rewards of appreciating the taken-for-granted behaviors that over time become quite costly to the family budget and financial goals.

The reflection process noted realizes step 5, "assessment of alternatives." Do the game nights that the family chooses over going to the movies have intangible rewards in addition to the reduction of entertainment expenses? Does the family walk after dinner help everyone to connect in a no-cost way even if the walk is limited to 20 minutes?

With a family collective goal of limiting expenses or increasing income, step 6, "selection of best alternatives" can assist the family in adopting new habits. At the very least, an increased awareness of the resources that are available can lead the family to steps 7, "action or implementation of alternative," and step 8, "evaluation of action and problem-solving process." The short-term needs to increase income and/or reduce expenses can lead families to becoming very creative in accomplishing their goals.

An appreciation of the resources that they do have available is heightened. The taken-for-granted habits of stopping at the local ice cream shop instead of eating the ice cream that is already at home in the freezer are noticed. Stopping at the fast-food restaurant for dinner or treating yourself to a drive-through cup of coffee are additional habits that over time can become costly. All of these suggestions require careful consideration, planning, and discussion to achieve the commitment of how the existing resources a family has available will be used.

Step 8 can even lead families to decide to continue the new habits. Discussion, self-disclosure, conflict management, and decision making are the communication processes by which navigating the family problem-solving loop will be achieved. The heighted awareness of how resources are used can increase appreciation for what the family already has in material goods. Intangible rewards such as family time together playing games instead of going to a movie can also create more emotional closeness and family satisfaction because of the time spent together.

Back to the Family Budget and Income Statements

The structure of a budget and income statement is the same. (Refer to tables 4.1, 4.2, and 4.3 for examples of the 1-month April, Jackson family budget, the three-month Jackson family budget, and the Jackson family income statement.) First the income sources are listed, then the list of expenses. It's helpful to see the "good" source of income before looking at what can be thought of as "the bad and the ugly" of expenses. Remember, we are remaining optimistic in this process that at first can be daunting, arduous, and plain "just not fun." It will get better, so keep going.

The upper, or first, part of the budget and income statement forms shows income from two sources: **active income** received from earnings, bonuses, or consulting, and **passive income** generated from investments, royalties, tax refunds, or rents. Total income from both sources is summed at the end of this section.

The second section provides a list of expenses in two parts: **nondiscretionary expenses** that represent the needs of your required obligations in the form of rent or mortgage payments, utilities, gas, car payments, insurance, and **discretionary expenses** that consist of wants or purchased items like jewelry, Starbuck's coffee, movie tickets, and a meal at a restaurant.

The total expenses, calculated as the sum of these two items, is listed at the bottom of the second section of the budget or income statement. Finally, the difference between total income and total expenses is recorded at the bottom of the statements. If total income exceeds total expenses, the amount is recorded as a surplus, money that is available to save or be used to further pay off debt. Surplus funds may also be used for discretionary purposes such as taking a vacation; however, care should be taken to see whether these additional funds might be better used to meet family financial goals. One contemporary indicator of the current misunderstanding of appropriate uses for surpluses in resolving financial planning issues is how many Americans view their April income tax refunds. In terms of a financial budget and income statement for April, many families will receive a tax refund, which generates a one-time surplus. The following sample income statement for the Jackson family in April serves to illustrate how items are recorded on an income statement and the generation of surpluses due to a tax refund.

TABLE 4.1 Jackson Family Budget Statement
From April 1–April 30, 20__

INCOME	
Active Income (based on earnings, bonuses, and consulting)	
Salary	$5,500
Tax Refund	$2,500
Passive Income (based on investments, interest, royalties, tax refunds, dividends, and rents)	
Dividend income	$ 350
Interest income	$ 25
Total Income	**$8,375**

EXPENSES	
Nondiscretionary expenses (based on needs, those things that you absolutely have to have)	
Rent	$2,300
Utilities	$ 500
Insurance	$ 750
Gas	$ 400
Food	$ 750
Cellphone/cable contract	$ 150
Clothing	$ 100
Charitable contributions	$ 300
Discretionary expenses (based on wants, those things that you can live without)	
Entertainment	$ 150

Dining out	$ 100
Total Expenses	**$5,500**
Net surplus or deficit	**$2,875 [Surplus]**

In this example, the Jackson family's April surplus is due to the $2,500 refund they received on their taxes. How did this refund come about? Let's consider withholding taxes that are deducted from your paychecks.

Every pay period, whether it's weekly, twice a month, or monthly, requires an employer to withhold an amount to pay for your income taxes that are due to the federal government and, in some states, state governments from your paycheck. Some states do not collect state income taxes, others do. The total annual withholding taxes are due at the end of the calendar year. On December 31, the end of the calendar year, the Jackson family is required to pay taxes based on their income earned during the year.

If the withholding tax taken from your paychecks during the previous calendar year (i.e., 2019 taxes are based on 2018 earnings) does not meet the actual tax bill that you owe, the difference will be due on April 15. If you paid too much withholding tax from the federal and/or state taxes, you will receive a tax refund. In our current example, if the Jackson family paid too little, they will owe taxes. If they paid too much, they will receive a tax refund. In this case, the Jackson family will get $2,500 as a tax refund because the amount withheld was more than what was needed to pay this year's tax.

A tax refund should not be considered a bonus, but rather a payment in recognition that you overpaid your taxes for the year. Withholding is a type of forced savings representing a monthly amount taken out of earned income to assure that most of the taxes due will be paid. The $2,500 tax refund is the return of a savings amount that was not needed to pay taxes for the year.

Unfortunately, many Americans do not understand tax refunds as a savings vehicle and proceed to spend refunds like they were some type of bonus. If the family has identified retirement savings or paying off loans as intermediate or long-term financial goals, then using at least part of a tax refund to help reach these goals would be more beneficial in keeping with their financial plan. One possible explanation for this phenomenon may be the lack of financial planning within the household, which avoids discussing appropriate uses for one-time money such as a tax refund. At the end of the day, the family might still decide to use the tax refund to make a discretionary purchase, but with a financial plan at least they will have made this decision understanding what the implications are to their money allocation.

Table 4.2 provides the three-month, April to June, budget statement for the Jackson family. This budget is based on estimates the Jackson family made relating to the income and expenses expected over that 3-month period.

TABLE 4.2 Jackson Family Budget Statement for 3 Months
April 1 to June 30 20__

INCOME	April	May	June
Active income			
Salary	$5,500	$5,500	$5,500
Tax refund	$2,000		
Passive income			
Dividend income	$ 350		
Interest income	$ 25	$ 25	$ 25
Total Income	**$7,875**	**$5,525**	**$5,525**
EXPENSES			
Nondiscretionary expenses			
Utilities	$ 350	$ 200	$ 350
Insurance	$ 750	$ 150	$ 150
Gas	$ 400	$ 450	$ 500
Rent	$2,300	$2,300	$2,300
Food	$ 750	$ 650	$ 575
Cellphone/cable	$ 150	$ 150	$ 150
Clothing	$ 100	$ 150	$ 75
Charitable contributions	$ 300	$ 300	$ 300
Discretionary expenses			
Entertainment	$ 150	$ 200	$ 150
Dining out	$ 100	$1 25	$ 150
Total Expenses	**$5,350**	**$4,675**	**$4,700**
Net Surplus or Deficit	**$2,525**	**$ 850**	**$ 825**
	Surplus	Surplus	Surplus

According to this sample three-month budget, the Jackson's largest surplus will occur in April. The estimated $2,535 surplus is the result of a projected tax refund of $2,000 coming in that month. In order to understand the actual refund that the Jackson's receive, we can review the following income statement for the month of April showing the actual realized income and expenses.

TABLE 4.3 Jackson Family Income Statement for the Month of April
April 1 to April 30

INCOME	April
Active income	
Salary	$5,500
Tax refund	$2,500
Passive income	
Dividend income	$ 350
Interest income	$ 25
Total Income	**$8,375**

EXPENSES	
Nondiscretionary expenses	
Utilities	$ 500
Insurance	$ 750
Gas	$ 400
Rent	$2,300
Food	$ 750
Cellphone/cable contract	$ 150
Clothing	$ 100
Charitable contributions	$ 300
Discretionary expenses	
Entertainment	$ 150
Dining out	$ 100
Total Expenses	**$5,500**
Net Surplus or Deficit	**$2,875**
	Surplus

In this instance, the $2,875 actual surplus is a bit higher than the $2,525 projected in the April budget, due in part to the higher $2,500 tax refund that came in. The budget estimated a $2,000 refund, but the Jacksons received $2,500 or $500 more in income.

IDENTIFYING AND RESPONDING TO THE FAMILY'S FINANCIAL POSITION

A balance sheet tells us about the family's **financial position** from past financial decisions in acquiring possessions and financing its operations. Table 4.4, the Jackson family balance sheet on April 30, is an example of a family financial sheet. The title at the top of the balance sheet states the date when the evaluation is being made, for example, "Jackson Family Balance Sheet as of April 30." This means that all items on the balance sheet will be listed at their current value as of that date, in this case April 30th.

TABLE 4.4 The Jackson Family Balance Sheet as of April 30th

What the Jackson Family Owns	
Checking account at the Coast Guard Credit Union	$ 7,000
Savings at US Bank	$ 2,500
Current value of 2015 Mazda 6 (45K miles)	$ 14,500
Estimated value of jewelry	$ 1,000
Retirement accounts	$ 85,000
Furniture, clothes and housewares	$ 15,000
Home purchased 7 years ago	$177,500
Total of all possessions: A	**$302,500**
What the Jackson Family Owes Others	
Chase credit card balance	$ 3,500
Home mortgage loan (outstanding balance)	$ 80,000
Current loan balance on auto loan	$ 9,500
Total of the Jackson Family's obligations to others: B	**$ 93,000**
The Jackson Family's Net Worth (wealth position): A – B	**$209,500**

The balance sheet first lists what a family owns from purchased goods that are used to support family activities. Items such as a home, car, savings accounts, retirement accounts, investments, furniture, books, and jewelry are examples of what may be found on the balance sheet. If you were completing a balance sheet on January 1 and owned a 2010 Toyota Corolla with 120,000 miles on it, then you would list it as one of your possession's worth about $6,000. You can determine a car's current value by doing an Internet search for cars with the same year, mileage, and comparable features using the Edmunds, Kelly Blue Book, Auto Trader, or NADA websites.

The next item found on the balance sheet is the obligations the family has to others. Loans, outstanding credit card balances, and lease payments are examples of what the family owes to others. If you financed your 2010 Toyota and have an outstanding loan balance of $2,000 as of January 1, that figure would be listed as an obligation. Outstanding loan balances can be found by calling the bank, credit card company, or student loan service firm that carries your debts.

Once you have identified and recorded the items you own, and what you owe others, you can calculate net worth by subtracting the items you owe from what you own. For example, if you owned $12,500 worth of items and owed $7,500 to others, your net worth would be $5,000 (i.e., $12,500 – $7,500). **Net worth** is a measure of your overall wealth. It is the amount of household value left over if you were to sell what you own to completely pay off what is owed others. The Jackson family has a net worth position of $93,000 as of April 30th.

Over time, a family will want to make financial decisions that increase net worth. Additional net worth gives a family greater ability to meet its obligations to others. Banks, and savings and loans and credit unions will look at your net worth as an initial measure for determining whether you qualify for a loan. As a family, growing net worth demonstrates that you are accumulating owned resources that can be used to meet future financial goals. For example, if one intermediate and long-term goal is to provide an educational savings fund to meet future college expenses, then increasing savings in this area each year will result in a larger amount of owned resources, in the form of savings, to reach this goal.

Reviewing a current balance sheet allows family members to understand their net worth position and develop strategies for increasing it. There are three ways a family can grow net worth. If the family is able to generate greater income over time and then use those funds to add to what it owns, net worth will increase. In this instance, what you own goes up while what you owe others stays the same, so the difference in the form of net worth increases. Income can expand. Either active income rises due to more money coming in from salaries, bonuses, tax refunds, and/or earnings from consulting, or passive income generates more cash from investments through dividends or interest.

A second way net worth can go up is if the value of what a family owns increases. If the family has stocks, bonds, artwork, or jewelry and any one of those items increases in value, then net worth can grow. The increase in net worth is similar to what happens when income rises, but in this case, the growth is due to an appreciation in what is owned. Not all owned items are the same when it comes to increasing in value. For example, the value of artwork and jewelry really depends on finding a willing and able buyer who is enthusiastic about paying a much higher price for these items than what they were originally purchased for. Another impediment to selling these items is the lack of a readily available market for transacting sales. Due to these factors, personal property items are considered to be illiquid or less able to immediately convert into cash.

In contrast, the ownership of financial instruments such as stocks and bonds are liquid because they can be bought and sold each day in an open market to convert into cash. Another distinguishing feature of stocks and bonds is that they can produce intermediate income in the form of dividends and interest while waiting for them to appreciate. Most personal property, with the exception of rental property that generates rental income, does not generate incremental income over time. Generally, any return from personal property comes at the time of sale should the price received be greater than what was paid to acquire the item.

The third and last method for increasing net worth is by reducing obligations owed to others. If what you own remains the same, but what you owe others goes down, then net worth will rise. In the most extreme case, if you had no obligations to others, then the balance sheet would have the value of what you own on the left, a zero amount for what you owe others, and net worth would be entirely what you own.

Some families seek this type of balance sheet as a long-term financial planning goal at the time of retirement. The rationale for such a choice is that at the time of retirement you will be leaving employment and not have much in the way of active income to make loan payments. Any loan payments made during retirement is most likely to come out of passive income in the form of retirement investments, which may vary significantly in value over time. Having little or no debt in retirement provides for a more stable financial picture by alleviating the need to have nondiscretionary loan payments in the budget. Table 4.4 is an example of the type of information found on a family balance sheet.

The Role Financial Statements Play in the Communication Process

All of these financial discussions and decisions lead us back to the communication strategies for initiating and maintaining productive talking within the family. Conversations that families have about money and how their resources will be used can overcome the stigma of the taboo topic of money. Families who do not talk about or are not even aware of how money-related decisions are made can perpetuate the mystique of money. Fear can grow from what is not known, and making money decisions based on lack of information, planning, and talking can lead to disastrous financial choices. Our perspective is that it's better to try to talk about the sometimes-difficult topic of money than to make your best guess on how to proceed.

Financial statements are essential for understanding the family's current financial position, how decisions have been made in the past, and what areas of financial decision making might offer ways to improve family net worth. A frank, objective, and fruitful conversation about family finances begins with an evaluation of a budget, income statement, and balance sheet. While it takes time to identify items and assign values to what is reported on the family's financial statements, there can be no meaningful discussion of financial choices without those documents. Once a family goes through the process of developing financial statements, the process of updating them will become easier to accomplish. Family members will be knowledgeable about what goes into the statements, where to get the data, and how it is reported to allow for an accurate appraisal of net worth position.

A later chapter will present ways to further evaluate and use financial statements to create action plans that incrementally move toward meeting the family's financial goals.

CHAPTER SUMMARY

After reading this chapter you should be familiar with what goes into creating a budget, income statement, and balance sheet, as well as how they may be used to initially assess a family's financial position. Several communication processes, including the family problem-solving loop, were applied to these steps of the financial planning process.

SAMPLE RESPONSE TO CASE STUDY 4
Getting a Picture of Our Finances

Bill and Melinda can begin by separating out those items they own from those that represent what they owe to others. The items they own along with their current value are listed in table 4.5.

TABLE 4.5 Bill and Melinda Parks Family Balance Sheet on September 15

What the Bill and Melinda own	
Savings at the credit union	$ 5,000
Checking account balance at the bank	$ 7,000
Certificate of Deposit (CD) at the credit union	$10,000
Estimated value of jewelry	$ 1,500
Retirement accounts [Bill: $5K, Melinda: $8K]	$13,000
Furniture, clothes and housewares	$ 2,500
Current value of 2012 Toyota Camry (47K miles)	$12,000
Total of all possessions: A	**$51,000**
What Bill and Melinda Owes Others	
Credit card balance	$ 5,000
Student loans (outstanding balance, Bill: $20K, Melinda: $5K)	$25,000
Current loan balance on auto loan	$ 5,500
Total of the Jackson Family's obligations to others: B	**$35,500**
The Jackson Family's Net Worth (wealth position): A – B	**$15,500**

The total of what Bill and Melinda own, $51,000, less the total of what they owe others, $35,500, is $15,500, their current net worth position.

Bill and Melinda should be commended on being able to save $15,000 (e.g., $10,000 in a CD, and $5,000 in the savings account). They have also done well in keeping their credit card and auto loans at a manageable level (i.e., the sum total of these two loans is $10,500, which is less than the $15,000 in savings.) Going forward, they should seek to reduce their student, auto, and credit card loans. Reducing what they owe others will decrease the amount subtracted from what they own and, as a consequence, increase net worth. At the same time, if they can continue to add more money to what they own, by adding to their retirement plan or increasing funds for their savings account, net worth will also rise.

Bill and Melinda have a fairly new car with relatively low mileage, but at some time they will need to find a replacement when the car is older and has higher mileage. Consequently, they should consider placing money into a car savings fund for a future auto purchase without having to have much in the way of an auto loan. Such a strategy would allow them to increase savings, which can then be used to purchase another owned item, in this case, a good used car later on.

Another way they could increase their net worth is by reducing expenditures on their wants, such as football tickets, dining out, or vacations. The idea would be to look at ways they might get the same experiences at a lessor cost. For example, they could attend one or two fewer football games by watching them on TV. A vacation closer to home where transportation costs are less could still provide activities and sightseeing offers for an enjoyable experience. Bill and Melinda could have an in-home dining experience where they research a favorite dinner entree online and replicate it in their own kitchen. Additionally, they could check out a highly rated movie from the library rather than renting a newer one through Redbox, Netflix, or Amazon Prime. A small amount saved each month going into a savings account or reducing student loan debt can add up over time and make meaningful additions to net worth.

SELF-CHECK QUESTIONS

True/False

1. An income statement is a long-term financial planning document that is used to assess family net worth.

2. Financial statement analysis is a uniform, consistent, and objective method for assessing a family's short-term and long-range financial decision making.

3. Budget and income statements are short-term financial documents that allow families to discuss and decide what expenditures will be made in relation to household income.

4. A balance sheet is a longer-term oriented financial document that shows what the family owns in the form of assets over what it has in debts or liabilities that are owed to others.

5. A nondiscretionary expenditure would be the purchase of a two-week vacation on the island of Maui during spring break.

6. A discretionary expenditure would be the purchase of two tickets to the Milwaukee Bucks NBA playoff game for $250 each.

7. When making a discretionary purchase, it is important to determine whether you may be creating a nondiscretionary expense such as occurs when buying a two-year cellphone contract.

8. A balance sheet provides information over a period of time, so reported items are based on their average values during that time frame.

9. As a family, growing net worth demonstrates that you are accumulating owned resources that can be used to meet future financial goals.

10. Personal property, such as a sterling silver set of dinnerware, is considered to be a possession with great liquidity that can be readily converted into cash.

Multiple-Choice Questions

1. Financial statement analysis involves identifying and recording financial information that permits an assessment of how well the family is

    a. keeping expenses within the level of income it's receiving.

    b. growing what it owns in relation to what is owed others.

    c. having meaningful discussions about financial goals.

    d. all of the above.

    e. only a and b.

2. A budget is sometimes referred to as a proforma income statement, because

    a. it is a forward-thinking document that lays out what a family intends to spend in relation to income that it expects to receive.

    b. it gives the net worth position.

    c. it provides financial information as of a point in time based on current market conditions.

    d. it shows what is owed others.

    e. it reports actual income over expenditures.

3. A discretionary expenditure is

    a. the payment for an obligation such as monthly utilities.

    b. the payment for a good or service that can be classified as a need.

    c. the payment for a good or service that can be classified as a want.

    d. the payment for a good or service that is within the family budget.

    e. the payment for an investment that will produce intermediate cashflows such as dividends.

4. Budget and income statements are short-term financial documents that allow

    a. families to determine their net worth position.

    b. families to discuss and decide what expenditures will be made in relation to household income.

    c. families to discover what they owe to others in the form of debt obligations.

    d. families to identify and record the value of what they own.

    e. families to develop a mission statement.

5. Which of the following are nondiscretionary expenditures?

    a. The purchase of a Willie Mays 1961 baseball card in mint condition

    b. Buying a two-year membership for Netflix

    c. Paying the premium on your health insurance

    d. a and c

    e. b and c

6. Which of the following represents what a family might own as found on a balance sheet?

    a. The home mortgage

    b. A generation-4 Apple watch

    c. The current outstanding balance on a Capital One credit card

    d. A 1-year Amazon Prime membership

    e. All of the above

7. If your financial budget for the last month shows that you had $3,500 in income and $3,450 in expenses, then

 a. you have a deficit of $50, which means that you underspent your budget.

 b. you have a surplus of $50, which means that you overspent you budget.

 c. you have a deficit of $50, which means that you overspent your budget.

 d. you have a surplus of $50, which means you underspent your budget.

 e. none of these.

8. One of the ways you could increase your net worth would be to

 a. borrow money from the bank to make nondiscretionary purchases such as a vacation in Belize.

 b. buy lottery tickets because the chances of winning favor those purchasing them.

 c. increase income by taking on a part-time job or developing a small business that generates additional earnings.

 d. pay down loans with the goal of eliminating them completely.

 e. c and d.

9. If you had $15,350 in owned items and $10,250 in obligations to others recorded on your balance sheet then

 a. you have an income surplus of $5,100.

 b. you have a net worth position of $5,100.

 c. you have a deficit of $5,100.

 d. you spent more money long term than you took in from income.

 e. you have too much student loan debt which you need to eliminate

10. An example of a passive income source would be

    a. dividends from stocks that you own.

    b. interest income from the savings account at your credit union.

    c. forced savings received from a tax refund for overpayment of last year's taxes.

    d. all of the above.

    e. only a and c.

Essay Questions

1. Describe the short-term financial statements that may be used to assess what a family spends in relation to what it receives in income and tell how they differ.

2. Explain the basic elements to a balance sheet and why it is important to understanding a family's long-term financial prospects.

3. What are the differences between nondiscretionary versus discretionary expenditures and how they can be used to help families live within a budget?

4. Explain how a surplus or deficit on an income statement can impact what is reported on a balance sheet and ultimately whether net worth goes up or down.

5. Tell how you would use information from the budget, income, and balance statements to assist a family wanting to increase net worth over time. What would be some helpful guidelines for having family discussions to avoid financial problems that could negatively impact net worth creation?

SECTION 3

THE APPLICATION AND ACTION PLAN

5

NOW YOU'VE DONE IT!
CREATING AN ACTION PLAN

LEARNING OBJECTIVES

After reading this chapter, you will be able to do the following:

1. Develop family financial goals

2. Describe how conflict can help the family discuss its goals to gain convergence and/or consensus about the family financial action plan

3. Describe how setting family financial goals incorporates a family's financial risks

4. Describe and assess the types of financial risk

5. Identify the process for defining, creating, and implementing family action plans that are in keeping with their values and goals

6. Identify when and how the family financial mission statement should be updated

---

CASE STUDY 5

Establishing Short-Term, Intermediate, and Long-Term Financial Goals

In chapter 3, we introduced Tim and Karen, a newlywed couple, and addressed how they could establish a shared set of family values to write a family mission statement in their family life cycle. As you recall, a family mission statement is helpful in focusing the family on what values are most important to them. Doing so influences how this newly committed couple will use their monetary resources.

Tim will be working in the Twin Cities, while Karen embarks on earning a medical degree from the University of Minnesota. During this period, their source of support will come from Tim's job, some parental support, and additional student loans for Karen. At the end of Karen's training, she will need to complete an additional three to five years of residency training. Every year there are many more medical school applicants than residency positions in the United States. As a consequence, Karen will need to move to where ever she is able to attain residency. Tim would like to complete an MBA degree to improve his career choices but is willing to delay his education until Karen finishes medical school. They would like to start a family, but only after Karen has finished her third year of medical school and completed the Step 1 exam, a critical test in securing residency.

Now, in chapter 5, we continue the discussion of how they use the family mission statement in exchanging ideas about short-term, intermediate, and long-term financial goals that reinforce the values found in their family mission statement. As you read chapter 5, contemplate on the short-term, intermediate, and long-term financial goals that Tim and Karen should establish that reflect the shared values noted in their family mission statement.

FAMILY FINANCIAL GOAL SETTING: SHORT-TERM, INTERMEDIATE, AND LONG-TERM GOALS

This section discusses characteristics of short-term, intermediate and long-term goals, strategies for developing goals in relation to family's mission statement, and shows how goals may be prioritized and ranking conflicts addressed. In chapter 3 the concept of creating short-term, intermediate and long-term goals was introduced. Now we present material on the practical aspects of preparing, ranking, executing and resolving conflicts related to family goal setting. Financial goals represent measurable outcomes that a family would like to accomplish within a reasonable and specific period of time. After completing the mission statement, the next step to the financial planning process is to identify short-term, intermediate, and long-term goals.

Short-term goals, likely to be realized within a year or less, address current financial issues that are required to maintain and sustain the family. Preparing and executing a budget, paying bills on time, finding a job, and obtaining suitable housing close to work are examples of short-term goals that help perpetuate the family.

Intermediate goals, from one to five years, represent objectives that lead to improved financial health for the family. Results from achieving intermediate goals allow members to witness and receive encouragement from how the financial planning process works and lead to better decision making. Selecting and purchasing a reliable, affordable car, successfully saving money for the down payment toward the purchase of a home, and reducing student loan debt by 40 percent are all intermediate goals that, when accomplished, demonstrate planning, commitment, and dedication to the financial planning process.

Long-term goals represent a family's future financial aspirations. Long-term objectives such as saving and accumulating sufficient funds to retire, taking an extensive vacation, paying half of the cost of an undergraduate education for your children, or extinguishing your home mortgage loan require consistent, persistent, teamwork and faith in the financial planning process.

There are two ways for family members to discuss and determine their short-term, intermediate, and long-term financial goals. One forward-oriented method has family members first discussing what short-term goals need to be met first, followed by conversations concerning intermediate objectives and then longer-term goals. Initially, the family focuses on what issues need to be addressed within the next year to sustain and improve finances. Once a set of short-term goals has been determined, intermediate goals can be discovered by considering financial objectives that are likely to take between one to five years to accomplish. Financial objectives that require 5 or more years to complete are deemed long-term goals.

After developing a set of goals for each time frame, the family determines whether each goal

- is financially measurable and can be attained within a year;
- supports a value or principle found in the mission statement; and
- is still desirable and yet to be attained.

If a goal fails any of these criteria, the family would reject it in favor of the other goals it has discovered.

A second backward-looking approach is to have the family review the mission statement and prepare a list of long-term, aspirational financial goals. To set the stage, family members might consider the question, "What long-term financial goal would make you happy?" Having developed a set of goals that requires more than five years to achieve, family members could consider the intermediate goals that might be necessary to realize for each longer-term goal. For example, if one of the longer-term goals is to buy an affordable three-bedroom, ranch-style home in Nashville, Tennessee, what would be some intermediate financial objectives to help the family reach this goal? Saving money for the down payment on a mortgage loan, creating and monitoring the family financial statements (balance sheet, and budget and income statements) used by banks to approve a loan, and identifying housing features and neighborhoods are some intermediate steps a family would need to complete to successfully achieve its long-term housing objective.

In similar fashion, a set of short-term goals that link to intermediate goals could be uncovered by having family members consider what current milestones might move the housing goal forward. Creating a budget and sticking to it, researching neighborhoods online, and determining the radius around home and schools that are ideal for the family are examples of short-term goals that relate to intermediate-term family housing objectives.

With a set of short-term, intermediate, and long-term family objectives, a necessary final step of goal setting is to prioritize the financial objectives in each time category. By rank ordering goals within each time frame, the family can weigh the relative importance of each objective when allocating financial resources. For example, if the intermediate goal, save enough money for the down payment on a home, has higher rank than payoff one half of our student loans in five years, then excess funds created by spending less money than what was earned would go to a down payment fund over making an additional student loan payment.

The ranking of longer-term goals is likely to change with family circumstances over the financial planning life cycle. For example, if paying off the home mortgage was a high priority in the early years of marriage, it may be of lessor priority 20 years later. By continuing to pay monthly payments on a 30-year mortgage, the balance will be completely paid off in ten years. Twenty years into a marriage, however, a couple in their 40s may need to increase funding to achieve their retirement savings goal. Directing excess dollars into retirement savings, rather than more rapidly paying down a mortgage, may be a more preferable choice. A review of the ranking of short-term, intermediate, and long-term goals should occur as part of the re-evaluation and updating of the financial planning process.

One approach to having the family discuss new rankings is to have each family member rank individual goals within each time frame, short term, intermediate and long term. The rank numbers would be from 1 to N, where N represents the total number of goals within a category. For instance, if there are five short-term goals, then a family member would rank them from 1 to 5. The lowest number would represent the highest ranked or most important goal. If buying a new car is your highest priority, then it would have a ranking of 1. Within each time frame, a family member can use a rank number only once. If you have five short-term goals, each goal would receive a unique number between 1 and 5. Totaling these family member rank numbers for each goal produces a summary rank score. Goals that have the lowest sum total would have the highest family ranking, while those with higher scores would be ranked lower. Table 5.1 is an illustration of what a summary rank table might look like.

TABLE 5.1 Summary Rank Total for the (Family Name)'s Family Goals

	Family	Member	Ranking		
	Jim	Mary	Nancy	Judy	Totals
Short-term goals (< 1 yr)					
Create/Monitor financial statements	1	1	2	4	8
Plan 10-day vacation	4	3	1	2	10
Increase retirement contribution 10%	3	2	4	3	12
Review/Purchase healthcare coverages	2	4	3	1	10
Highest to lowest ranked short-term goals	**Family ranking**				
Create/Monitor financial statements	1				
Plan 10-day vacation	2 [Tied]				
Review/Purchase healthcare coverages	2 [Tied]				
Increase retirement contribution 10%	4				
Intermediate-term goals (1–5 years)	Jim	Mary	Nancy	Judy	Totals

(continued)

TABLE 5.1 Summary Rank Total for the (Family Name)'s Family Goals *(cont.)*

Save money for home down payment	1	1	2	1	**5**
Save $10K in an individual retirement acct.	3	3	4	4	**14**
Complete a 2- year weekend MBA	2	2	3	3	**10**
Provide piano lessons for Nancy	5	4	1	2	**12**
Complete 90K mile car maintenance	4	5	5	5	**19**

Highest to lowest Intermediate-term goals	**Family ranking**
Save money for home down payment	**1**
Complete a 2-year MBA	**2**
Provide piano lessons for Nancy	**3 [Tied]**
Save $10K in an individual retirement acct.	**3 [Tied]**
Complete 90K mile car maintenance	**5**

Long-term goals (> 5 years)	**Jim**	**Mary**	**Nancy**	**Judy**	**Totals**
Sufficient retirement funds to retire at 65	1	2	6	6	**15**
Own a home	2	1	1	1	**5**
College fund: Half tuition each child	3	3	4	5	**15**
Vacation home	5	6	3	4	**18**
Purchase well- equipped, affordable SUV	6	5	2	3	**16**
Accumulate $500K in investments	4	4	5	2	**15**

Highest to lowest long-term goals	**Family ranking**
Own a home	**1**
Sufficient retirement funds to retire at 65	**2 [Tied]**

Highest to lowest long-term goals	**Family ranking**

College fund: half tuition each child	**2 [Tied]**
Accumulate $500K in investments	**2 [Tied]**
Purchase well-equipped, affordable SUV	5
Vacation home	6

Now that the short-term, intermediate, and long-term financial goals have been identified through the hard numbers, let's consider the topic of interpersonal conflict that may happen at any point in the financial planning process. From there, we will move on to the topic of making a family action plan that reflects the family mission statement.

Interpersonal Conflict

Our values are demonstrated in the behaviors we exhibit and the choices that we make. How we spend money and make purchases reflects what is important and valued by us. If on payday you pay your housing bills, buy groceries, and put $50 into a savings account, these choices demonstrate that you value housing, food, and having some money for a longer-term goal. Conversely, if you spend your paycheck on a new outfit, fragrance, and shoes before paying your immediate bills, these actions also reflect that you value your personal appearance above your basic living needs. No judgment is intended in these two examples. The point is that how we prioritize our spending and actually spend the money reflects what we value. Sometimes we say that we want to save for intermediate or long-term goals but our actions do not follow. Saying and doing must be consistent to be successful in your financial goal setting and achievement.

As you have navigated the process of rank ordering your family's short-term, intermediate, and long-term goals, you have probably had many discussions about what is most important to you individually as well as part of a couple or family. Differences of opinion inevitably occur. Let's consider more fully how to approach the conflicted situation.

In chapter 1, you learned about the concept of interpersonal conflict. As you recall, according to Hocker and Wilmot, *conflict is an expressed struggle between at least two interdependent parties who perceive incompatible goals, scarce resources, and interference from others in achieving their goals* (3). The terms in the definition were broken down to describe what *interdependence, incompatible goals, scarce resources,* and *interference from others* mean in a conflicted situation (Hocker and Wilmot 3–10). In this section, the conflict goals are identified so that as you work through conflict you can be purposeful in discussing the differences of opinion.

When we think about conflict, we need to be cognizant of the TRIP goals. This acronym stands for

T: The **topic** of disagreement. "What topic are we disagreeing about?"

R: The **relationship** that exists between the two (or more) people having the conflict. "Who are we to each other in this conflict?"

I: The **identity** that the individual people in the conflict have of them-selves within the conflict. "Who am I in this conflict?"

P: The **process** by which the people in the conflict discuss the disputed topic. "How will we discuss this problem?"

Let's consider an example. You and your friend are having a conflict about punctuality. You are always on time for activities, having coffee, and study sessions. Your friend, however, usually arrives about 10 minutes after the appointed time for meeting. In this example, the topic (T) of the conflict is "punctuality." Punctuality is the outside concept that is removed from you and your friend. Yet, punctuality, or the lack of it, has now become an issue in your relationship (R) to each other. How is your relationship affected by your punctuality and your friend's lack of it? "Who are the two of you together in this relationship?" is an important question to answer in the (R) goal. If you have a different sense of relational meaning to your friendship than your friend, this lies squarely in the (R) goal.

Third, the (I) goal is about your own personal identity in this situation. How is your identity affected by your friend's chronic tardiness? What is your friend's identity in this situation? Do you have a sense that your friend does not respect your time and, hence, does not respect you? Is your friend unaware how the lack of punctuality affects your identity? Does your friend think that his or her time is more important that yours? If so, how does this affect his or her identity?

Finally, the (P) process goal refers to the way that you and your friend talk about your conflict. Remember, in order for interpersonal conflict to exist it must be expressed. Otherwise, it is an internal frustration or struggle but not an interpersonal conflict. Conflict requires talking about the disputed topic. The process goal can be face-to-face discussion, e-mail, text messaging, and phone calls, to name a few examples. The media by which you discuss your conflict will affect how the discussion goes. We have all heard of people having texting "wars" on social media that can quickly escalate the conflict and move it in a different direction from the original conflict topic. The process by which you communicate is vitally important to the outcome of the conflict.

Applying the TRIP goals to developing a couple or family financial action plan can be very useful. Writing down the points of disagreement such as "saving for a $150,000 home" and "buying a first car for our 16-year-old teenager" can be helpful when establishing the time frame for when the financial goal will be achieved. Perhaps your 15-year-old teenager is hoping that on his or her 16th birthday a new car will be in the driveway. You and your partner, on the other hand, may prefer "saving for the $150,000 house."

These two separate financial goals reflect the values of both parties. Thinking about and clarifying who you are to each other in your family and your own personal identities in relationship to each other (the R and I goals), will help you focus on how these separate goals are valued and prioritized in the minds of the conflict parties.

Determining how you will discuss the conflict topic is an important consideration as well. Limiting the discussion to family meetings or family conversations is an important "rule" to establish. If the teenager is allowed to negotiate separately with each parent (if there are two parents), it encourages the teenager to "play one parent against the other parent." Likewise, if the parents continue their discussion of saving for the $150,000 house in the absence of the teenager, the conflict can possibly escalate.

As we have considered the concepts of self-disclosure and the three levels of "risk" in telling someone information about ourselves that would not otherwise be known along with interpersonal conflict, these tools for discussion and decision making cannot be over emphasized. The willingness to take risks, reveal what we individually and as part of a couple or family value, and talk through areas of disagreement will help your financial planning progress.

During the times when you think that the financial planning and communicating process is "stuck," revisit the family problem-solving loop and/or the family life cycle stages to check if adjustments are needed in the overall development of your family. Perhaps a resident child is now moving out to attend college. The family system will change as this transition takes place. The planning for the college education, if it occurred soon enough in the financial plan, will see its fruition of saved funds for a major educational expense.

Additionally, the new college student who moves out of the house will have an effect on the overall family system. Other children may want to move into their sibling's room. Perhaps the now vacant room may be preserved for holidays and vacations for your college student's return home. Or, a totally new use for the room may be deemed appropriate. Any of these choices will affect the family and may require the family to review its current stage of development as well as its financial plan.

SETTING FINANCIAL GOALS THAT INCORPORATE A FAMILY'S FINANCIAL RISKS

Family **financial risks** represent unpredictable events that can significantly impact family finances. These risks can be classified into two categories: property risks and non-property risks.

Property risks include loss of a home or personal property due to fire, tornado, hurricane, flooding, or earthquake; automobile damage due to an accident or fire; and loss of personal property due to theft. Non-property risks consist of loss due to poor health, unemployment, poor financial advice leading to low investment returns, liability damages assessed against a family member, or the pre-mature death of someone in the family.

A family can either recognize financial risks and develop ways to mitigate against financial loss or ignore risks and hope they never occur. Ignoring risks will likely lead to the family being unprepared for a financial risk when it occurs. It may also result in the family facing a financial crisis should resources be inadequate to meet the costs of dealing with a property or non-property loss. Addressing financial risks will require that the family identifies risks before they happen and develops strategies for dealing with those risks should they occur.

Table 5.2 provides a listing of family property risks and methods for addressing these financial risks.

TABLE 5.2 Property Risks and Methods for Addressing Them

Type of financial risk	Risk-management technique for addressing it
Loss of home due to fire, wind, or earthquake	Homeowner's insurance
Damage or total loss of a home due to flooding	National Flood Insurance program offered through FEMA
Loss of personal property in the home	Homeowner's insurance
Loss of jewelry, artwork, stamp/coin collections	Bank safety deposit box for small items, additional homeowner's coverage for the rest
Damage to your car due to collision with another car	Personal auto policy with collision coverage
Damage to your car due to means other than collision with another car	Personal auto policy with non-collision coverage

Homeowner's insurance is a cost-effective way to cover damage or loss of a home due to the perils of fire, wind, or earthquake. For a relatively small premium homeowners can be covered for the full value of their house. In most cases, a lending institution will require that a property owner maintain coverage on his or her home at least equivalent to the amount of the home mortgage. The homeowner's policy also covers personal property lost due to fire, wind, or earthquakes and offers some insurance for losses from theft.

If the family owns valuable jewelry, artwork, or collections, such as stamps, coins, or baseball/football memorabilia, then additional property insurance in the form of a rider on a homeowner's policy would be needed to cover theft of these items. One alternative to buying a rider might be to pay to have the items put in a bank safety deposit box provided they are small enough to fit in a box.

One type of peril that is not covered by a homeowner's insurance policy is loss due to flooding. Flood insurance has become almost a necessity for homeowners to have due to climate change. Some parts of the United States, once thought to have little likelihood of flooding, have become places where flooding has occurred with disastrous results. The National Flood Insurance program is provided through the federal government through the Federal Emergency Management Agency (FEMA). Before purchasing a home, it is best to investigate whether the property you are interested in is in a flood plain.

One other helpful coverage found in a homeowner's policy is additional living expense insurance. This coverage provides much needed funds for a family to live in a different place while their home is being rebuilt should their home be completely destroyed from fire, wind, or earthquake.

A personal auto policy provides coverage for physical damage to your own car from either colliding with another vehicle or events involving something other than collision with another car. A car owner can elect to have either collision or non-collision coverage or both. Collision insurance will reimburse you if you get into an accident with another car. Collision insurance, however, will not cover instances where your car gets damaged as a result of something other than colliding with another car.

What are these types of situations? Here is a brief, but by no means exhaustive, set of circumstances where non-collision coverage would be needed:

- You are driving down the road and hit a deer or wild turkey
- The truck in front of you loses an unsecured paint can from the flatbed, which strikes the front end of your car
- You are going through a construction site and the truck carrying gravel in front of you drops some stones, which shatter your front windshield
- On a wintry evening you slide off the road and into the ditch, taking out the front end of your car when hitting an ice embankment

In addition to the physical damage protection, a personal auto policy also offers coverage that will pay for your use of a rental car during the period when your car is being repaired.

Now that the types of property risks and the methods for dealing with them have been described, we'll move on to Table 5.3 that gives a list of non-property risks along with methods for dealing with them.

TABLE 5.3 Non-Property Risks and Strategies for Addressing Them

Non-property risk	Risk-management technique for addressing it
Liability due to personal injury to a visitor at the home	Homeowner's insurance, liability coverage
Liability due to personal injury to another from a car accident	Personal auto policy, liability coverage

(continued)

Non-property risk	Risk-management technique for addressing it
Healthcare costs related to illness, preventive care, or pharmaceutical drugs	Health insurance
Premature death of a family member	Life insurance
Disability of a family member	Disability insurance
Unemployment	State unemployment insurance and a six-month personal emergency fund
Poor financial advice	Thoroughly vetting qualifications and services of a financial advisor Use of index funds with low fee structure

One of the major financial risks a family faces is liability due to personal injury. Liability loss occurs infrequently but can result in significant financial damages. The two main sources for liability risk relate to the home you live in and the car you drive.

If you own or rent a home, liability risk comes from potential injury to visitors to the property. For example, if you neglect to clear the walkways after a snowstorm, and a postal worker slips and falls on the snow and ice, you could be financially liable for the worker's healthcare costs, days off work, and any long-term pain from this incident.

When a car is being driven, the owner is liable for any damages to another party due to negligence. If a family member were found to be at fault for an accident causing either physical damage to another person's car or personal injury to another person, the owner of the car would be financially liable for all damages. The most cost-effective way of addressing these liability risks is to purchase adequate amounts of liability coverage in the family homeowner's and personal automobile insurance policies.

Standard liability coverage is about $300,000; however, many families are purchasing $500,000 worth of coverage or more due to increases in liability judgments over the past decade. Since liability claims occur infrequently, the cost of coverage for these losses is affordable. In addition, few families would have the financial resources to pay a $300,000 unexpected personal damage settlement.

The other large loss financial risk is health care costs should a family member become seriously ill. Today, the three ways families obtain healthcare coverage are through an employer, individual purchase through an insurance company or exchange, or member share. When looking for coverage, families should first zero in on a plan that provides adequate catastrophic medical care coverage. The standard amount of large loss coverage for major medical insurance is at least $1 million. Having attained that amount of coverage, families should make sure the plan offers medical care in the specialties and areas that are needed by family members.

Another family financial risk is the early death of a family member. If the family is dependent on a member who dies prematurely, the flow of funds to pay family expenses will be reduced. The best method of addressing this risk is the purchase of life insurance.

The first type of life insurance is term insurance. Term life insurance is an affordable way to handle this risk, allowing a young couple beginning a family to inexpensively buy a large amount of coverage.

The second type of life insurance that is often overlooked when assessing financial risk is disability insurance. Necessary family income can be lost if a working member becomes disabled for a long period of time. Disability insurance may be offered by an employer. Alternatively, individual disability insurance policies can be purchased from a private insurer.

Disability insurance is most needed when parents are relatively young, have a growing family, and do not have a robust retirement savings. As parents get older and closer to retirement, they are likely to have greater funds to meet the challenge should one of them become disabled.

In the last decade, unemployment or underemployment has become a matter of increasing concern for families due to the 2008 recession. States provide some assistance in the form of unemployment insurance. Yet, the coverage is minimal and not for a long period of time.

To be adequately covered for this type of risk a family should seek to have saved six months' worth of wage income at a minimum. In an emergency, these resources can be accessed along with funds in a retirement account. It is important to the family that savings and retirement monies be invested to generate good long-term returns.

Finding a financial advisor who can offer honest, helpful, and beneficial assistance is not easy. If a family decides to seek help from a financial advisor, a list of characteristics sought in the financial advisor, the duties and functions that the financial advisor is expected to provide, and the cost or fees that will be incurred to secure such an advisor should be discussed and developed. Talking with other friends and family members about experiences and who they believe are good advisors can be equally helpful.

One way to obtain a reasonable rate of return without incurring large investment fees is to invest in index funds. Index funds, like the S&P 500 Index, offer a financial return based on the overall health and expansion of the U.S. economy. Index funds are not managed funds. This means that index funds do not have the large advisory fees that other funds do. Mutual funds have advisory fees. Knowing that index funds exist is important for your being able to decide what may be the most cost-effective means to invest. It is beyond the scope of this book to go into depth about investments and the types of funds available to consumers. However, in the next chapter, a section on continuing communication and financial planning provides references and suggestions on how to become better informed about investing.

THE PROCESS FOR DEFINING FAMILY ACTION PLANS IN KEEPING WITH VALUES AND GOALS

An **action plan** may be the activity when adjustments may take place because the most important couple or family values have come to the surface. Family action plans are an outgrowth of setting goals in keeping with the mission statement. With a ranked set of goals in each time category, members can discuss what current steps will move the family forward toward meeting those objectives. Short-term goals have immediacy and require development of action plans for the coming year. Intermediate goals provide an impetus to take incremental actions that increase their likely achievement within five years. Longer-term goals help the family focus on what short-term and intermediate action plans are needed to come ever closer to accomplishing these broader, notable targets.

Action plans take into account a goal's priority ranking, as well as the financial resources required to complete it. Higher-ranked goals that have actions involving limited financial costs should be initiated first. In the previous example, creating and monitoring family financial statements is the highest short-term goal. It involves family members taking time to obtain financial information necessary to prepare a balance sheet, budget, and income statements and then periodically review results to make budget changes. This set of actions involves very little financial costs other than the paper, pencil, and calculator used to develop and record the information. However, the results of these actions may lead to more cost-effective financial purchases that increase savings. This in turn may help in the achievement of an intermediate goal, such as having the down payment to buy a home.

Action plans should also take into account goals that are equally ranked but have different financial resource requirements. In our earlier illustration, there were two short-term goals with equal ranking, plan and go on a 10-day vacation, as well as review and purchase health insurance. The short-term goal, to plan and go on a 10-day vacation, will require a financial expenditure within the next year, characterized as a want as opposed to a need. Depending on transportation, housing, and entertainment expenses, the actions to achieve this goal might cost anywhere from a few hundred to several thousand dollars.

The equally ranked short-term goal of reviewing and purchasing family health care coverages may involve a varying financial outlay. The review of health care plans involves few resources other than the time to read and evaluate the current coverage and obtain information on competing policies. The purchase of affordable and sufficient health insurance for family members, however, may involve a significant outlay of funds as a need rather than a want.

Through the action of evaluating and selecting affordable and comprehensive medical coverage, the family may save money that can be used in meeting other financial goals. An annual review of health care coverage may be worth the effort for two other reasons: (a) to know what is covered, and for how much, before filing a claim and (b) to be able to coordinate coverage if two parents are working and have access to employer-sponsored health insurance. Ultimately, money that can be saved when completing short-term goals allows for additional resources in attaining intermediate and long-term objectives.

With intermediate or longer-term goals, meeting a goal may represent smaller steps toward accomplishing that goal. If the family has as a long-term goal, such as purchasing a home, then having the intermediate goal to raise funds for a down payment moves the family forward to eventually purchasing its own home. Reaching a longer-term goal requires a commitment to completing short and intermediate action plans to achieve the long-term objective. A family will not be able to purchase a home if it doesn't accumulate funds for a down payment and develop the financial statements required by the lending institution to make a mortgage loan.

The initial family discussions about goal attainment should focus on what each goal means in terms of its accomplishment. A question to consider is "How many financial resources will it take to meet the goal?" For example, with a home purchase, how much does the family want to accumulate for the down payment: $10,000, $15,000, or $20,000?

The amount saved in a down payment will dictate how much home a family can buy. If the down payment is going to represent 10 percent of the cost of a home, then a $150,000 home needs a $15,000 down payment. By meeting the intermediate goal of saving $15,000 for a home purchase, the family can then move toward buying a home.

The relevant action plan might be to set aside either a set dollar amount per month or a percentage of salary income annually into a savings account for accumulating the $15,000 down payment. Family discussions need to center on what financial resources are required to achieve each goal and what actions will deliver those dollar amounts from the family budget. During these discussions, returning to the family problem-solving loop to help guide the conversations will help focus the family on the goal. In this regard, the Chinese proverb is worth noting, "A journey of a thousand miles, begins with a single step" (Lao-Tzu).

Once action plans have been developed, the family can begin completing them to see how well they are working to reach each goal. Action plans may change due to new family circumstances, alterations in the economic landscape, or decisions to alter an original goal. Changes within a family will occur with the birth of children, job or career changes, health issues, and/or emerging care needs for aging parents. Financial downturns, downsizing by an employer, or a promotion that involves moving to another city represent unforeseen economically driven events that can alter the trajectory of an action plan to meet a specific goal.

In some instances, family members may no longer feel committed to goals that have been set earlier when there was less information about the benefits and costs of them. For example, if the family sets as a long-term goal saving money for a summer vacation trip to Yosemite National Park seven years from now, there may be better, less-expensive alternatives that present themselves 5 years later when children weigh in on what most interests them most. If the family is living in Nashville, Tennessee, and spending time in the Great Smokey Mountains, taking a trip up Skyline Drive in the Shenandoah Mountains would involve less travel and could include visits to several historical sites that might be preferable to hopping on a plane to San Francisco, renting a car, and driving to Yosemite. Saving money on air travel could also free up additional funds for better hotel/resort accommodations. A strategy to explore national parks near Tennessee first and then have the children help plan transportation and accommodations for a trip to Yosemite when they are older could save money and provide practical experience on how to plan and budget travel expenses.

At the end of every year, action plans should be re-evaluated and updated on the basis of new information and an assessment of how well each action plan is working toward achieving the family's intended goals. For instance, if you are saving to reach a $10,000 goal for the down payment on a home in five years and you have been setting aside $2,000 each year, then three years from now you might have $7,000 in your fund based on contributions and investment returns. At that point, a family might change its action plan to put $1,500 in the down payment fund for the next two years to reach the $10,000 goal, continue the annual $2,000 outlay and overfund the account, or put in $2,000 this year and a smaller amount the following year to reach the $10,000 target.

Sometimes adjustment of the action plans can be made to fine tune the financial plan. If a goal is being met sooner than the original time frame, then some of the money earmarked for the original goal could be reassigned into meeting other goals that need additional funds. Conversely, if the time frame for attaining a goal has not been adequately calculated, the family will need to discuss and decide how to alter the action plan to improve the chances of meeting the goal in a timely fashion.

THE PROCESS FOR CREATING AND IMPLEMENTING FAMILY ACTION PLANS

1. Using a ranked set of goals, discuss current actions and financial resources that permit achievement of short-term, intermediate, and long-term objectives.

2. Concentrate discussion on actions to meet short-term goals with current financial resources.

3. Discuss what actions and financial allocations will enhance the likelihood of reaching intermediate and long-term goals.

4. Talk about the linkages and trade-offs between intermediate and long-term actions and financial allocations and come up with ideas to achieve them.

5. Re-evaluate and update your action plans based on new information for executing the plans.

Updating the Family Mission Statement

Even though the family mission statement is an agreement that lays out the values, aspirations, and life perspectives that guide family decisions long term, it must also be flexible enough to adjust to changing conditions that affect the family. As the family evolves and changes through the stages of the family and financial life cycle, adjustments are inevitable. The family mission statement should be reviewed at least once every year as part of the evaluation of action plans and how goals are being met. However, if there are events that significantly alter family goals, such as unemployment, death of a spouse, or a job change that requires moving to a new location, then a review and update of the mission statement is in order. Having a family conference to analyze the mission statement within this context allows family members to discuss how to address difficult issues within the context of shared values and principles. It is likely that when developing an initial mission statement families are unaware of the types of circumstances they may face years later. A family mission statement should be a living document that changes to fit any new challenges faced by family members going forward. Family members have talents, needs, personalities, and perspectives that impact family decision making on financial matters. The family mission statement is a document that should be flexible enough to incorporate the unique characteristics and aspirations of family members. If through family discussion it becomes apparent that the mission statement lacks a particular value or principle needed to improve family relations, then it should be changed for the betterment of all.

The family mission statement writing and the establishment of short-term, intermediate, and long-term financial goals provide an excellent time to revisit the difference between a need and a want. By now you are very aware of the difference between needing an item, service, or other resource to live. Housing, food, clothing, transportation, insurance, and educational opportunities are needs to maintain a stable economic lifestyle. Cell phone contracts, cable, Netflix, restaurant dinners, and buying the latest perfume trend are wants. While the cell phone is becoming an increasingly important part of our technological and digital lives, the type of phone that you use can become a want. So too is it with clothing. If having the trendiest jeans or active wear for school or leisure time is on your have-to-have list, these are wants. You can go to class and work out with less expensive clothes on your back, if you want to remain within your budget and save for future financial goals.

The activities that have been discussed in the current and past four chapters are all to help a couple or family discuss and make decisions about what is most important to them in terms of values. These values, then, drive the monetary choices that the couple or family will make to achieve their goals. Differences of agreements will surely arise. This is when the communication concepts in chapter 1 should be revisited as a reminder of how to navigate the discussions to make decisions.

CHAPTER SUMMARY

Chapter 5 revisited the family short-term, intermediate, and long-term financial goals, described how interpersonal conflict can help families clarify and make decisions about their financial action plan, identified the financial risks that all couples and families face and ways to address them, explained the process for defining, creating, and implementing family action plans that are in line with values and goals, and pinpointed when and how the family financial mission statement should be updated.

SAMPLE RESPONSE TO CASE STUDY 5
Establishing Short-Term, Intermediate, and Long-Term Financial Goals

Tim and Karen can exchange ideas about short-term, intermediate, and long-term financial goals that reinforce the values found in their family mission statement. At this point, they should be able to identify parts of the family mission statement that directly relate to the financial goals they wish to achieve. If that is not the case, then they will need to either drop the financial goal or alter the mission statement.

Under the current circumstances, Karen and Tim might consider the following financial goals:

Short-term goals

- Develop a budget
- Investigate and decide on location, cost, and size of housing,

- Start to pay down Tim's student loan
- Discuss ideas on how to minimize the cost of medical school for Karen
- Start funding a retirement account

Intermediate goals

- Karen completes medical school and obtains residency
- Have at least one child
- Eliminate Tim's student loan debt
- Continue funding a retirement account
- Support Tim in getting promotions

Long-term goals

- Purchase a home in the area where Karen will serve as a doctor
- Have at least two children, if possible
- Fund retirement accounts for Tim and Karen
- Set aside funds for a college education fund

The family mission statement offers a framework for allocating financial resources. It, however, will need to be revised when circumstances change. For example, if children arrive, then the financial mission statement may be altered to emphasize the values and responsibilities parents have with child rearing. Revisiting the mission statement at least once every two years will permit family members to revisit the values and directions that are important them. It also will allow family members to consider changes to the statement that may better reflect new perspectives about what is important. Tim and Karen should use their mission statement when discussing significant family life cycle events that may impact family financial planning. For example, upon the completion of Karen's medical degree, she could be required to move to a new city to complete her residency. Such a transition might impact Tim's employment, the financial goal of owning a home, and/or Tim's goal of obtaining an MBA. The values and priorities found in the mission statement should provide perspectives on how these issues may be addressed. Discussing the sacrifices some family members might have to make in reaching a particular family goal, means there will be better understanding of the importance and reasons for the sacrifices being made. In the absence of such a conversation, and without the benefit of a mission statement, decisions about future employment, housing, and education are likely to be made unilaterally and in the moment, leading to misunderstanding and discord.

SELF-CHECK QUESTIONS

True/False

1. The initial step toward creating and defining the family mission statement begins with identifying shared short-term, intermediate, and long-term financial goals shared by family members.

2. Financial goals represent measurable outcomes that a family would like to accomplish within a short period of time, the sooner the better.

3. Short-term, intermediate, and long-term goals are separate objectives that have no linkages to each other; if you pursue an intermediate goal, it has nothing to do with achieving a long-term objective.

4. With intermediate or longer-term goals, opening actions toward meeting a goal may represent smaller steps toward accomplishing an objective.

5. Family action plans are an outgrowth of setting goals in keeping with the mission statement.

6. At the end of every year, action plans should be re-evaluated and updated on the basis of new information and an assessment of how well each action plan is working toward achieving intended goals.

7. Interpersonal conflict should be avoided to keep the family financial process going.

8. Rank ordering the family goals is one of the steps in the family action plan process.

9. Liability risk associated with owning a home or driving a car is a relatively small financial risk that can easily be handled from the family savings account.

10. As part of the process for defining, creating, and implementing family action plans, there should be a discussion about the linkages and trade-offs between intermediate and long-term goals and the financial allocations to determine ideas to achieve them.

Multiple-Choice Questions

1. Which of the following represents an intermediate financial goal?
    a. Creating a budget for the next year

b. Paying off the outstanding balance on the credit card account each month

c. Paying off your student loan in the next four years

d. Putting away $3,000 a year into a retirement account in order to retire 45 years from now when you turn 65

e. Buy a $250,000 house in seven years

2. One of the benefits of rank ordering financial goals is

a. helping the family prioritize the relative importance of each goal when allocating financial resources.

b. helping the family negotiate the terms of their next vacation.

c. helping the family identify its values.

d. helping the family assess their individual goals.

e. helping the family to revisit their mission statement.

3. The forward-oriented method for a family to discuss and determine short-term, intermediate, and long-term goals would be to

a. wait until a short-term, intermediate, or long-term issue arises and then address it.

b. set long-term goals that family members can look forward to should intermediate goals be met.

c. have family members first discuss what short-term goals need to be met first, followed by conversations concerning intermediate objectives, and then longer-term goals.

d. develop intermediate goals that allow the family to move forward with short range actions to attain long-term objectives.

e. define a set of action plans that move the family forward to achieve intermediate and long-term financial goals.

4. The TRIP name is an acronym for goals in a conflict situation. Which of the following are the full terms for each letter?

a. Topic, relativity, ideas, and procedures

b. Topic, relevance, ideals, and process

c. Topic, reliability, ideas, and process

d. Topic, relationship, identity, and process

e. Topic, relevance, identity, and procedures

5. The personal identity (the "I" goal) that you have in a conflict is reflected in which of the following questions?

   a. "What is the issue we are disagreeing about?"

   b. "How will we talk about the issue?

   c. "Who am I in this conflict?"

   d. "Who are we to each other in this conflict?

   e. "What is the rule for discussion and decision making in this conflict?"

6. Financial risks can be expressed in two categories: property and non-property. Which of the following is an example of a property risk?

   a. Health care costs

   b. Loss of your home due to a flood

   c. Disability of a family member

   d. Unemployment

   e. Premature death of a family member

7. One of the methods for addressing property risks for the loss of your home due to fire, wind, or earthquake is by which of the following?

   a. A rider on your personal insurance policy

   b. Homeowner's insurance

   c. FEMA (Federal Emergency Management Agency)

   d. National Flood Insurance program

   e. Life insurance

8. The process for creating and implementing family action plans include all of the following EXCEPT

   a. the use of ranked set of goals to discuss the actions and resources needed to achieve the financial objectives.

   b. concentrating on actions to meet only the short-term goals.

   c. discussing what actions and financial allocations will enable reaching the intermediate and long-term goals.

   d. talking about the linkages and trade-offs between intermediate and long-term goals and ideas on how to achieve them.

   e. re-evaluating and updating the action plans based on new information.

9. The purpose of a family mission statement includes all of the following EXCEPT

    a. it is an agreement that lays out the values, aspirations, and life perspectives that guide family decisions long term.

    b. it is an agreement that is flexible.

    c. it is an agreement that should be evaluated every six months.

    d. it is an agreement that should be considered a living document.

    e. it is an agreement that is unique to every family.

10. According to the book, which of the communication models and/or concepts are helpful when a family's discussion and decision making become "stuck?"

    a. The family problem-solving loop

    b. The family life cycle stages

    c. Self-disclosure

    d. Interpersonal conflict

    e. a and b

Essay Questions

1. Describe the two approaches for families to discuss and determine their short-term, intermediate, and long-term financial goals. Use examples to illustrate the respective approach.

2. Define *interpersonal conflict* and describe how the TRIP goals can help families discuss their differences of opinion. Use an example of an interpersonal conflict to illustrate each of the TRIP goals.

3. Identify three of the financial risks that families can face. Identify the categories of the risks and the strategies by which the risk can be addressed.

4. How do the financial risks faced by a family influence their family action plans?

5. Setting up a six-month emergency plan was identified as a strategy to address a non-property financial risk. What communication strategies would you use to convince your family to make the six-month emergency plan a short-term goal?

6

REFLECT AND RE-EVALUATE
REGULAR CHECK-UPS FOR YOUR ACTION PLAN

LEARNING OBJECTIVES

After reading this chapter, you will be able to do the following:

1. Describe how family financial planning can create family stability and satisfaction

2. Describe how conflict management skills can become a part of the continuing family financial planning process

3. Describe how communication can facilitate the ongoing process of family financial planning

4. Describe how continuing family financial education can energize family financial planning

5. Apply the technical and communicative processes by which a family creates and re-evaluates a family financial plan

---

CASE STUDY 6
Reflecting and Re-evaluating the Family Financial Plan

Tim and Karen Turnbull, after 15 years of marriage, now have two twin daughters, Anne and June, both age 12. They live in a three-bedroom, two-bath, 2,600-square-foot home in Eden Prairie, Minnesota where Karen and Tim work. Tim is a senior computer software engineer in a Fortune 500 product development program. Karen is a pediatrician with a children's clinic near their home. Tim will be starting an executive MBA program at the University of Minnesota. Tim's company will pay for the cost of tuition. Tim will spend the next 12 months going to school and, as a consequence, not receive a regular salary. Once he earns his degree and returns to work, he will earn $200 more per month in salary in recognition of his MBA degree.

The twins, Anne and June, enjoy school and have developed interests in a variety of areas. They play the piano and like tennis, two activities they hope to continue through high school. Both children are drawn to academic subjects. Anne writes poetry and excels in math and French. June has artistic talent, particularly drawing, is good at computer coding, and also has an aptitude for math. The twins have shadowed their parents. June has an interest in getting more involved in computer programming. Anne has expressed a desire to explore careers in medicine.

While it is too early to determine where the girls might go to college or what area they would study, Tim and Karen have put $8,000 in a college investment account. This money is invested in the S&P 500 Index fund. They hope to contribute $2,000 each year into this account and increase the amount to $3,000 annually once they pay off their own student loan debt five years from now. The following is last year's income statement for the family.

TABLE 6.1 Turnbull Family Income Statement for the Period January 1, 2018 to December 31, 2018

INCOME:	
Tim's salary	$75,000
Karen's salary	$125,000
Dividend and interest income	$3,000
Total annual income: A	**$203,000**
EXPENSES:	
Federal and state income taxes	$24,000
State property taxes	$5,050
Student loan payments	$4,538
Mortgage payments	$24,349
Utilities	$2,750
Transportation expenses	$3,678
Food	$5,328
Auto insurance	$3,575
Homeowner's insurance	$2,322
Medical malpractice insurance	$9,358
Retirement contributions	$40,500
Charitable contributions	$10,500
Credit card expenses	$32,346
Children's educational fund	$2,000
Total annual expenses: B	**$170,294**
Net income: A – B	**$32,706**

The Turnbull family balance as of the end of 2018 is shown in table 6.2.

TABLE 6.2 Turnbull Family Balance Sheet as of December 31, 2018

Assets (what they own)		Liabilites (what they owe others)	
Home	$365,000	Mortgage Loan	$320,682
Savings, CD	$10,000	Credit card balance	$2,522
Checking	$3,561	Student loan debt	$25,376
Retirement accounts	$155,347		
Investment accounts	$30,000		
Education account	$8,000		
Autos	$12,000		
Personal property (jewelry, furniture, etc.)	$10,000		
Baldwin baby grand piano	$4,500		
Total Assets: A	**$598,408**	**Total Liabilities: B**	**$348,580**
Net Worth (wealth): A – B			**$249,828**

Given the Turnbull's financial life cycle changes, what areas of their financial plan need to be updated? How might family discussions now differ from the ones that occurred when Anne and June were younger? Why would conversations about Tim's going back to school for an MBA be important? What does his returning to school mean to the family budget?

FUNCTIONING FAMILY AND FINANCIAL PLANNING RELATIONSHIPS

Chapter 6 returns to the broader issues of communication and financial planning that were raised in the introduction and developed throughout this book. As you have learned, financial planning is an ongoing process in family relationships. Working together in a communicatively supportive environment will make the reflection and possible revision of the family's financial action plan more effective. There may be financial difficulties that families will face, but with the understanding of how communication plays an important part in family financial planning, families will be better able to work through the process.

As part of the reflection process, this chapter will address how families may reconcile differing views on how to implement and apply the financial process, as well as work through conflicts that may arise when completing a financial plan. Specifically, we will consider conflict management strategies and restate the importance of family adaptability and cohesion.

In a general sense, there is no such thing as a "normal" family. Instead, family communication theorists and scholars often use the terms "stability" and "satisfaction" as ways to gauge the functioning of a family. (Olson, et. al) The term **stability** refers to the expectation that the family relationship will continue. Having a "stable" relationship suggests that you anticipate, or expect, the relationship to continue and are confident in that assumption. An "unstable" relationship, on the other hand, creates a less-than-confident expectation that the relationship will continue. "On-again, off-again" relationships are a good example of an unstable relationship. For families, if a partner separates from the other partner, this creates instability for the entire family. Instability creates uncertainty and can raise the anxiety level of the whole family.

Satisfaction, a separate concept, describes the general fulfillment experienced in the family. Dissatisfaction implies that the family is not fulfilled. Figure 6.1 is a representation of how stability and satisfaction can help us see the overall functioning of the family.

FIGURE 6.1 Stability and Satisfaction Axes

	Stable	
Satisfying	Lasting relationships that are satisfying	Lasting relationships that are not satisfying
	Satisfying relationships that do not last	Dissatisfying relationships that do not last	Dissatisfying
	Unstable	

Source: David H. Olson, et al., from "Stability and Satisfaction Axes," *Families: What Makes them Work*. SAGE Publications, 1989.

The value of addressing the concepts of stability and satisfaction is that families that are dissatisfied because of financial problems, can become more aware of how and why the financial stressors are creating the instability and dissatisfaction. Stability and satisfaction, like many communication concepts, are symbolic representations of the ebb and flow of relationships. We don't necessarily feel the same way in our relationships at all times. The overall assessment of the two concepts is the goal.

The family financial planning activities and process that we have described throughout the book are ways that can help a family becomes more satisfied and stable. The specific financial documents (e.g., mission statement; short-term, intermediate, and long-term goals; budget; financial income statement; and financial action plan) that we have suggested you complete, have no doubt provoked discussion and decision making. Differences of opinion and conflict have been planned for and strategies to address them have been suggested through the introduction of communication concepts. The *interpersonal conflict* definition, TRIP goals, family problem-solving loop, and family life style stages are most notable. Yet, considering some the habits that are developed individually and as a family when in conflict may assist you in working through the conflict in productive and communication-based ways. There are ways to "fight" dirty and "fight" clean.

Fighting Dirty and Fighting Clean: Conflict Management Strategies

Fighting dirty means that a person wants to "win" the conflict at all costs. An "I-must-win-lest-I-lose" attitude is an apt adage for this approach. Here are just a few characteristics for fighting dirty:

- A person apologizes prematurely. Apologizing prematurely can shut down the discussion of the conflict topic. An apology may presume that the discussion is over because an "I'm sorry" statement has been made. The person who apologizes prematurely implies a dismissal of the conflict. Conflict arises, apology given, end of discussion.

- A person refuses to take the conflict topic seriously. If a person makes light of the topic, such as the family mission statement and values identification, then the impression is given that the activity is unimportant. An unwillingness to participate fully in the joint activity jeopardizes the entire discussion and decision making.

- A person throws in unrelated issues. Known as "gunnysacking," the strategy is to bring up unrelated topics and points of disagreement to escalate the attack. If the family is discussing the financial goals and a family member brings up "the time when," this suggests that the family member feels that his or her needs or wants were unmet. This can lead to a conversation about "the time when" rather than the financial goals under discussion.

- A person withdraws to avoid confrontation. When a person leaves the room or becomes silent, participation has stopped and so has the discussion. Avoidance is a conflict strategy. Avoidance delays discussion and decision making.

- A person withholds rewards from another person. Withholding affection, recognition, material things, or privileges are strategies for discipline. They are not helpful or productive strategies in conflict management.

Fighting clean provides a framework or guidelines for discussing the disputed topic. As you may have already observed, the authors like documents. There is value in writing things down so that all participants can look at what is written for consideration and discussion. Consider a meeting agenda as an example. A list of topics to be discussed at a meeting provides a guideline for moving the discussion along and making decisions. Fighting clean is similar in some of its characteristics:

- The family gives full expression to the positive and negative feelings related to the conflict topic. Knowing that the family will engage in giving all members a "full hearing" of their feelings is a supportive communication strategy. Respect and reciprocity grow out of giving and receiving a full expression of your feelings.
- The family allows the emotional nature of the topic to subside before discussing the topic. People who are emotional don't make good decisions. Neither do they contribute to productive discussions. An emotional outburst needs to diminish before conversations can occur.
- The family paraphrases each other's statements and arguments in their own words. Paraphrasing is a skill that conveys your understanding of another person's statement. Similar to content and relationship dimensions of communication that were discussed in chapter 1, paraphrasing expresses both the content and the emotion expressed in a message. As the listener, you reflect on both the content and the emotion you heard in the speaker's message. For example, Pam may express to her mother, "I'm so frustrated at work. Whenever it's near the end of the day, the department secretary asks me to take letters to the campus post office and I miss the bus." Pam's mother, when paraphrasing, might reply, "I understand that your supervisor gave you important work to complete just before the end of the work day. She knows that this means you have to take a later bus to go home. I can appreciate your frustration."
- Paraphrasing may slow down the discussion, but it clarifies both the content and the understanding of it. Paraphrasing helps create greater understanding during conflicts.
- The family expresses to each other that they want to help resolve the issue. Knowing that a positive outcome is regarded and supported by the entire family demonstrates respect. Maintaining respect for

each other, especially in conflict situations, contributes to more productive discussions when in conflict.

Families who exhibit appropriate self-restraint in their discussions, conflicts, and decision making are deemed more functional than those who don't. The level of stress and anxiety will be lessened when boundaries are made clear for respectful and productive conversations. This isn't to suggest that conflict should be avoided. Remember, avoidance is a conflict strategy. The conflict doesn't go away in the absence of talking about it. The point is that families who are purposeful in their conversations can more successfully reach decisions about their financial planning. The communication strategies and concepts that have been described can assist you in having more meaningful and productive discussions about financial matters and other family-related topics.

REGULAR CHECK-UPS FOR YOUR FINANCIAL PLAN

You and your family have been introduced to the entire family financial planning process with the completion of the family action plan. Navigating this six-part process has been important, educational, and probably challenging, at times. Money is a necessary resource. Your increased knowledge and planning have enabled you and your family to complete a big accomplishment. Congratulations!

The family financial plan is your culminating document for this process. Just like other important papers, there will need to be a scheduled **action plan evaluation** and, if needed, revision to your plan. The timing of this review is highly dependent on the family life cycle stage in which you find yourselves. As families change, a review of your plan is a good time to look at where you stand. Yearly check-ups are suggested. This can be done at the beginning of the calendar year, or you might select a fiscal year end, such as June 30, as the point when you will review the action plan. The financial planning process, along with the communication strategies, will become more familiar to you. The more you practice the skills, the better you will become at them.

CONTINUING COMMUNICATION AND FINANCIAL EDUCATION

You have learned a number of insights into communication and family financial planning in this book. Some information may have been new to you; other information may have already been known. More can be learned about communication and financial planning. As with any skill, such as playing an instrument or sport, there's always more to know and there are new techniques or ways of doing things. So too it is with communication and financial education.

Communication education can be gained through taking a course in interpersonal communication, family communication, and conflict management. Local universities and community colleges offer face-to-face and online courses. The purpose of this book was to introduce you to some basic communication terms and concepts. We barely scratched the surface, so to speak, about the discipline of communication. One of the advantages of learning more about communication is that you can apply the concepts immediately in your daily life. That's often an attraction for students of all ages to this vibrant discipline.

Book stores and Internet sources offer a myriad of popular literature about improving personal relationships and self-improvement. A number of basic course textbooks have been mentioned throughout the chapters and are listed in the bibliography. These are good introductory sources for beginning students of communication. Academic journals, such as *Communication Studies, Communication Monographs*, and *Journal of Communication Pedagogy* are sources of research-based communication studies that are geared toward advanced studies.

Over time, as part of a family's life stages, there may be new issues requiring additional understanding of financial concepts. If interest rates have declined, does it make sense to refinance the home mortgage? With more children should the family complete a home improvement project to expand living space or sell the existing home and buy a larger one? As the family grows should life insurance coverages be updated? Does it make sense to pay off student loans early or continue to make regular payments in order to deduct interest expenses off the federal tax return? If investment savings has grown to over $20,000, does it make sense to spend time investigating and buying good, quality, dividend-paying stocks? At what point does it make sense to engage the services of a financial advisor? What are the types and prices of such services?

Fortunately, there are many ways family members can obtain additional financial education on topics related to financial planning. There are whole sections of the library and bookstores devoted to financial and investment planning. Two texts, *Personal Financial Planning*, by Gitman, Joehnk and Billingsley, and *Personal Finance: Skills for Life*, by Vickie Bajtelsmit, are good references on topics related to financial planning. Magazines, such as *Money*, *Financial Planning Magazine*, *Kiplinger's Personal Finance*, *Better Investing*, *Consumer Reports*, the *Journal of Financial Planning* and the *Journal of the American Association of Individual Investors* offer articles that provide insights on financial planning issues.

Local community colleges and universities may offer evening classes in financial planning that can serve to update skills on financial topics. Financial institutions, such as banks, credit unions, and brokerage firms will periodically provide free financial planning seminars for clients.

In the area of investing, additional knowledge may be obtained by reading books, such as Benjamin Graham's *Intelligent Investor*, or *Buffettology* by Mary Buffett and David Clark, or joining a local investment club sponsored by the National Association of Investors Corporation. The NAIC is a nonprofit organization that was created in 1951 to help individuals learn about investing. A listing of local clubs by state and city is available on their Better Investing website.

Financial planning and communication are continuous learning and improvement processes. The abundance of resource materials for both of these areas of study should allow families to explore new ways to address financial issues, leading to better family conversations. The uniqueness of this book is that the authors have combined the two disciplines of communication and finance. This endeavor is meant to provide you with practical and doable guidelines for enhancing your talk about financial planning and taking action to improve your family's financial health and security.

FINAL REFLECTIONS ON COMMUNICATION AND FAMILY FINANCIAL PLANNING

One of the purposes of this book was to offer a communication framework for family conversations about finances. Our aim was to help you and your family move from seeing money as a "problem" to viewing money as the "path" to achieve your financial goals. The key to addressing financial issues is to have honest, fair, and productive family discussions about finances.

As you have learned, most of the financial planning decisions faced by families are the result of family life stages that include such events as entering into a committed relationship, having and caring for children, working, taking care of parents, securing retirement funds, and distributing wealth at the end of life. All of these family life stages require planning, budgeting, and, more importantly, communicating in order to reach these financial goals. Establishing your shared values; developing a family mission statement; knowing your short-term, intermediate, and long-term financial goals; understanding the functions of a budget and income statement; and knowing about and planning for risk have presented the opportunities for families to discuss and make decisions about how they will use their money.

We hope that *Communicating Finances in the Family: Talking and Taking Action* has assisted you to address the important relationship between communication and financial planning. The information presented will help you, whether you are part of a couple or a family, think, talk, plan, and negotiate the use of your money. Ultimately, we hope that you now understand how the tools of financial planning, along with the process of communication, can assist you and your family reach agreed-on financial goals to feel more secure and informed about finances.

CHAPTER SUMMARY

Chapter 6 described how family financial planning can create family stability and satisfaction along with how conflict management skills can become a part of the continuing family financial planning process. The ongoing process of family financial planning and communication was revisited. Opportunities and advantages of continuing communication and family financial education were described. The benefits of regular financial check-ups were described. Finally, reflections about communication and family financial planning were offered.

SAMPLE RESPONSE TO CASE STUDY 6
Reflecting and Re-evaluating the Family Financial Plan

A review of the Turnbull family balance sheet shows how past decisions have strengthened family finances and net worth over time. Initially, Tim and Karen started out with a large amount of student loan debt. Karen's medical education was significant; however, Tim's job covered family living expenses, and Karen's use of an in-state school helped lower the loan burden.

Salary income from Tim and Karen allowed those student loans to be reduced to the point where only $25,376 remains. While paying off these loans, steps were taken to build up retirement and investment savings and begin a college education fund for the twins. The value of their home, $365,000, is greater than their outstanding loan balance of $320,682 creating a favorable equity surplus that increases net worth by $44,318 ($365,000–$320,682).

Karen and Tim have kept their transportation costs low. They own autos worth $12,000 that are free of any loans. Maintaining and driving cars longer allows them to pay less for insurance, license, and registration fees. They can also save what would have been paid on an auto loan. The savings can go toward a future car purchase.

The income statement describes a family that is able to pay bills, save money, and purchase adequate insurance against unexpected financial risks. However, the family will need to discuss the following areas to see whether or how much the financial plan needs to be adjusted to changing circumstances:

- Once the student loans are paid off, how should money once used for that purpose be redeployed to other family financial goals?

- With Tim returning to school next fall, there will be a reduction in household income of $75,000. What changes should there be to the budget to allow the family to live comfortably for the next year while Tim completes his MBA?

- Now that Anne and June are older, will setting up household chores help them save money for college? Are there activities that might allow them to better explore and expand their interest in a potential career? Would summer camp experiences in computer coding for June and French for Anne start this process? If so, what areas of the budget will need to be reworked to free up funds for these educational initiatives?

- Given less salary income, the family should pay less in federal and state income taxes, and this might result in a year-end tax refund. If any tax refunds materialize, how should that money be allocated, to the college education fund, to investment savings, or paying down the mortgage?

- In addition to these financial issues, there are the emotional and time commitments of the family to Tim as he adjusts to being a graduate student at an older age. He may not have as many free hours to spend with the twins. Karen may be required to handle home finances as well as the transportation needs of June and Anne. What sacrifices will each family member make to allow Tim to successfully complete his education? How important is education as a value for all family members?

SELF-CHECK QUESTIONS

True/False

1. Families who exhibit appropriate self-restraint in their discussions, conflicts, and decision making are deemed more functional than those who don't.

2. Financial planning is an ongoing process in family relationships.

3. Working together in a communicatively supportive environment will make reflecting and revising the family's financial action plan more effective.

4. Family financial planning guarantees a stress-free financial life.

5. Normal families are the most functioning.

6. Family communication theorists and scholars describe families as functioning rather than normal.

7. Satisfied families are generally stable.

8. "Gunnysacking" is a strategy for fighting clean.

9. Paraphrasing, as a listener, reflects on both the content and the emotion you heard in the speaker's message.

10. Boundaries are not important when engaging in a conflict.

Multiple-Choice Questions

1. Which of the following describes a family that is able to pay bills, save money, and purchase adequate insurance against unexpected financial risks?

a. A budget

b. A mission statement

c. An initial action plan

d. An income statement

e. A revised action plan

2. On-again, off-again relationships are good examples of which of the following?

    a. Stable relationships

    b. Unstable relationships

    c. Functioning relationships

    d. Satisfying relationships

    e. Dissatisfying relationships

3. Which of the following might be used to gain additional information about financial planning topics?

    a. Reading a book from the local library on personal finance

    b. Asking your best friend for advice on what might be a good investment

    c. Joining an investment club sponsored by the NAIC in your area

    d. Reading magazines such as *Money Magazine* or the *Journal of Financial Planning*

    e. All of the above except b

4. When is it suggested that a family review and update their financial plan?

    a. When a family member wants to talk about how their favorite football team did on Saturday

    b. When a family member decides to take a nap during the family conference on fiances

    c. Whenever there is a life-changing event, such as the birth of a child, job change or healthcare emergency

    d. Once children go off to college

    e. b and c

5. Characteristics of a clean family fight is(are) when

   a. one family member brings up an unrelated issue to the financial topic being discussed.

   b. a family member becomes silent and remains silent when discussing a financial issue.

   c. a family member refuses to take financial planning seriously.

   d. the family gives full expression to the positive and negative feelings related to the conflict topic.

   e. b and d.

6. The communication skill that conveys your understanding of another person's statement is called

   a. self-disclosure.

   b. fighting clean.

   c. summarizing.

   d. clarifying.

   e. paraphrasing.

7. Paraphrasing includes two separate levels of response that you heard in the other person's message. The levels that are reflected back in your paraphrase are

   a. content and relationship.

   b. content and response.

   c. content and emotion.

   d. content and identity.

   e. emotion only.

8. Which of the following is an example of a paraphrase?

   a. "It'll be okay. Not to worry. It's only one movie."

   b. "Wow! It sucks to be you. You should re-evaluate who your friends are."

   c. "Too bad, so sad. Your friend is not treating you nicely."

   d. "Let's not talk about this now. It's late in the day. I think that you are tired and overreacting."

   e. "I can appreciate your frustration. Your friend's lack of punctuality made you late for the movie."

9. All of the following are good ways to learn more about communication and communication strategies with the exception of

    a. no further study about communication because you've been communicating all your life.

    b. taking a communication course at your local community college.

    c. reading popular literature about personal relationships.

    d. reading credible articles about communication on the Internet.

    e. maintaining a heightened awareness about the importance and ubiquitous nature of communication.

10. Which of the following is an example of gunnysacking?

    a. "I know that we are talking about the budget. Can we stop and talk about this a little more?"

    b. "Planning for the future is fine, but what about our immediate needs?"

    c. "With the exception of our insurance needs, our budget is looking pretty good."

    d. "Let's talk about my trip to the Ozarks. I don't really care about the budget."

    e. "I know that we are disagreeing about our health care needs, but what about my mother's housing needs?"

Essay Questions

1. Define the concepts of stability and satisfaction in family relationships. Illustrate how these concepts are helpful in describing functioning families.

2. Multiple strategies exist when engaging in a conflict. Define "clean fighting" and "dirty fighting" and describe two strategies for each category.

3. Identify and describe the two most helpful communication strategies for your family discussions about financial planning. The strength of your response depends on the thorough description of the communication strategies and your examples of them.

4. Describe the continuing communication and financial education opportunities that you will pursue. Identify the value for your family of continued learning in these two areas.

5. Describe the importance of regular check-ups for your family action plan. How are review and re-evaluation important to the overall family financial planning process?

Answer Key

CHAPTER 1

True/False

1. True
2. False
3. True
4. False
5. True
6. True
7. True
8. True
9. True
10. True

Multiple Choice

1. e. Only a and b
2. d. One that is spoken and expressed by talking
3. c. Has great risk because it involves telling information about ourselves that potentially may result in negative evaluation from another person
4. a. Leaving home as a single young adult

5. c. Developing adult-to-adult relationships between grown children and their parents

6. b. Consensus, accommodation, and *de facto*

7. b. Talking

8. b. Phase 2

9. d. Family roles

10. e. Family rules

CHAPTER 2

True/False

1. True

2. False

3. True

4. False

5. False

6. True

7. True

8. False

9. True

10. True

Multiple Choice

1. e. All of the above

2. a. During childhood

3. c. Paying the utility bill to heat the family home

4. d. Have a discussion at home, in a quiet place where all family members can participate in the conversation

5. a. Any purchase that is required in order to live a productive and useful lifec.

6. c. Families to avoid doing financial planning

7. b. Family members are afraid to learn about their financial position and confront what to do about it

8. a. Consider the needs, resources, goals, and abilities of all family members

9. e. b and c

10. b. Some family members may be unaware of financial planning decisions made on their behalf

CHAPTER 3

True/False

1. True

2. True

3. False

4. True

5. True

6. True

7. True

8. False

9. True

10. False

Multiple Choice

1. d. All of the above

2. a. Outlines core family values that can serve as a yardstick for measuring whether a particular financial decision either reinforces or detracts from a family's values

3. d. All of the above

4. d. All of the above

5. d. Occurs in the first step of the financial planning process when a family thinks about money and its uses within the family

6. d. All of the above

7. a. A periodic review and updating of the family mission statement

8. b. A short-term goal that can become an intermediate or long-term goal depending on the time needed to fully fund the down payment

9. c. A long-term financial goal

10. b. They can become second nature and with experience are completed more easily than when first initiated

CHAPTER 4

True/False

1. False

2. True

3. True

4. True

5. False

6. True

7. True

8. False

9. True

10. False

Multiple Choice

1. e. Only a and b

2. a. It is a forward-thinking document that lays out what a family intends to spend in relation to income that it expects to receive

3. c. The payment for a good or service that can be classified as a want

4. b. Families to discuss and decide what expenditures will be made in relation to household income

5. c. Paying the premium on your health insurance

6. b. A generation-4 Apple watch

7. d. You have a surplus of $50, which means you underspent your budget

8. e. c and d

9. b. You have a net worth position of $5,100

10. d. All of the above

CHAPTER 5

True/False

1. False

2. False

3. False

4. True

5. True

6. True

7. False

8. True

9. False

10. True

Multiple Choice

1. c. Paying off your student loan in the next four years

2. a. Helping the family prioritize the relative importance of each goal when allocating financial resources

3. c. Have family members first discuss what short-term goals need to be met first, followed by conversations concerning intermediate objectives, and then longer-term goals

4. d. Topic, relationship, identity, and process

5. c. "Who am I in this conflict?"

6. b. Loss of your home due to a flood

7. b. Homeowner's insurance

8. b. Concentrating on actions to meet only the short-term goals

9. c. It is an agreement that should be evaluated every 6 months

10. e. a and b

CHAPTER 6

True/False

1. True
2. True
3. True
4. False
5. False
6. True
7. False
8. False
9. True
10. False

Multiple Choice

1. d. An income statement
2. b. Unstable relationships
3. e. All of the above except b
4. e. b and c
5. d. The family gives full expression to the positive and negative feelings related to the conflict topic
6. e. Paraphrasing
7. c. Content and emotion
8. e. "I can appreciate your frustration. Your friend's lack of punctuality made you late for the movie."
9. a. No further study is needed about communication because you've been communicating all of your life
10. e. "I know that we are disagreeing about our health care needs, but what about my mother's housing needs?"

Glossary

Accommodation: letting others make the decision because discussion or continuing discussion is viewed as having no effect on the ultimate agreement.

Action plan: a concrete set of financial steps to meet desired financial goals determined in an organization's or individual's financial plan.

Action plan evaluation: an outcomes-based part of the financial planning process that involves determining how well a particular action plan is helping an organization or individual meet its financial plan goals within the context of a financial plan.

Active income: income received from earnings, bonuses, or consulting.

Adaptability: the ability to adjust to ever-changing family circumstances and experiences. Adaptability has four levels: rigid, structured, flexible, and chaotic.

Asset: a financial measure of what is owned by an organization or individual.

Balance sheet: a financial statement showing what is owned and owed to others and the amount of wealth accumulated by an individual or organization as of a point in time.

Budget: a short-term financial statement that projects income and expenses for an organization or individual over a period of time, sometimes referred to as a pro-forma income statement.

Cohesion: the emotional bonds that couples and families have. Cohesion has four levels: disengaged, separated, connected, and enmeshed.

Communication: a complex process through which we symbolically create and share messages and meanings with others.

Conflict-management strategies: Communication strategies used in conflict situations that assist in managing and resolving disputes.

Consensus: the most discussion-based level and democratic form of agreement.

Decision making: the process by which a choice is made. Three levels of agreement include consensus, accommodation, and *de facto.*

De facto: decisions that occur when an impasse has occurred. No clear agreement has been achieved through talking so a decision is made in order to move on.

Discretionary expenses: expenses other than nondiscretionary expenses, which represent financial costs to an individual or organization that may be forgone and still survive.

Family: a couple to multi-generations who live together and function to collectively create a stable, safe, and satisfying environment for its members.

Family and financial life cycle stages: the sequence of life stages that a family faces from birth to death that impacts financial planning decisions and communication about financial matters.

Family communication: the interactions that occur between couples and families over time.

Family dynamics: the cohesion and adaptability that exist between a couple or within a family that are expressed through communication.

Family life cycle stages: the sequence of life stages that a family faces from birth to death.

Family problem-solving loop: a guide to help families identify when disclosure and decision come together.

Family roles: patterns of behavior that are developed and enacted through communication between couples and within families.

Family rules: guidelines for living that help a couple or family function in day-to-day activities.

Family values: the ideals and principles mutually held by family members by which they wish to be identified.

Finances: funds that are available to meet specific needs.

Financial mission statement: a statement that outlines the values, aspirations, and guiding principles of an organization or individual that informs how financial goals and decisions will be made.

Financial planning: the deliberate process of determining how the use of money fits into the values of an individual and organization and the taking of steps to improve financial position in relation to those values.

Financial planning process: a six-step process for improving financial decisions in keeping with the shared values of an individual or organization consisting of (1) thinking about money and its uses; (2) determining short-term, intermediate, and long-term financial goals; (3) identifying, through financial statement analysis, the current financial position; (4) using information from steps 1 through 3 to create action plans to achieve financial goals in keeping with a mission statement; (5) periodic evaluation of the mission statement and financial goals; and (6) re-evaluation of the missions statement and goals to update the financial plan.

Financial position: the financial picture presented by examining financial statements involving the budget, income, and balance sheet statements of an organization or individual.

Financial risk: a situation or circumstance that gives rise to uncertainty about the financial position of an individual or organization.

Financial statement analysis: the process of examining the budget, income, and balance sheet statements of an individual or organization to determine their ability to meet current and future obligations, grow wealth, and make financial choices consistent with a financial plan.

Income statement: a short-term financial statement showing actual income and expenses over a period of time and whether an organization or individual has created a surplus or deficit in income.

Intermediate-term goal: a measurable financial goal that can reasonably be attained within a one- to five-year time frame.

Interpersonal conflict: an expressed struggle between at least two interdependent parties who perceive incompatible goals, scarce resources, and interference from others in achieving their goals.

Liability: a financial measure of the financial obligations of an organization or individual representing what is owed others.

Long-term goal: a financially measurable goal that can be met in five years or longer.

Money: a medium of exchange and store of value that can be used in exchange to obtain goods and services.

Need: a good or service an organization or individual requires in order to survive.

Net worth: a financial measure of what has been accumulated in wealth over a period of time, based on the calculation of assets minus liabilities on the balance sheet.

Nondiscretionary expenses: those expenses an individual or organization are required to incur to maintain survival or financial security.

Passive income: income generated from investments, royalties, tax refunds, or rents.

Pragmatics of human communication: Five principles that influence our view of communication that are based on a 1967 study conducted by Paul Watzlawick, Janet Beavin Bavelas, and Don D. Jackson.

Satisfaction: describes the general fulfillment experienced in the family.

Self-disclosure: revealing information to another person that he or she would not otherwise know. Self-disclosure has three risk levels: low, middle, and high.

Short-term goal: a measurable financial goal that can reasonably be met within a year.

Stability: refers to the expectation that the family relationship will continue.

Want: any good or service that is not a need, but rather something extra that can be purchased to enhance or bring pleasure to an organization or individual.

Works Cited

Allan, Graham., and Christian Gerstner. "Money and Relationship Difficulties." *Relating Difficulty: The Processes of Constructing and Managing Difficult Interaction*, edited by D. C. Kirkpatrick et al., Lawrence Erlbaum, 2006, pp. 81–100.

Bresciani, Alessio. "What Makes A Good Mission Statement," https://www.alessiobresciani.com/foresight-strategy/what-makes-a-great-mission-statement/. Accessed 8 November 2019.

Business Dictionary. "Values," www.businessdictionary.com/definition/values.html. Accessed 6 November 2019.

Caplan, Arthur. "Ten Years after Terri Schiavo, Death Debates Still Divide Us: Bioethicist," *NBC News*, March 31, 2015, www.nbcnews.com/health/health-new. bioethicist-tk-n333536. Accessed 8 March 2019

Carnes, Patrick. *Contrary to Love: Helping the Sexual Addict.* CompCare, 1989.

Clear, James. "Core Values List," jamesclear.com/core-values. Accessed 6 November 2019.

Derlega, Valerian.J. *Self-disclosure* . SAGE, 1993

Dew, Jeffrey, et al. "Examining the Relationship between Financial Issues and Divorce." *Family Relations Journal,* vol. 61, no. 4, 2012, pp. 615–628.

Epstein, Nathan B., Ryan, Christine E., Bishop, Duane S., Miller, Ivan W., Keitner, Gabor I. The McMaster Model: A view of healthy family functioning, 2003. In Walsh, Froma. Normal Family Processes: Growing diversity and complexity, 3rd ed. (chapter 21, pp. 581-607). Guilford Press, 2003.

Galvin Kathleen M., et al. *Family Communication: Cohesion and Change.* 10th ed., Routledge, 2019.

Gitman, Lawrence. J., et al. *Personal Financial Planning.* 13th ed., South Western Cengage Learning, 2014.

Hocker, Joyce. L., and William. Wilmot, *Interpersonal Conflict.* 10th ed., McGraw-Hill, 2018.

Hudson, Alison. "When Did Christmas Become so Controversial?" *Skeptoid*, December 19, 2013, skeptoid.com/blog/2013/12/19/when-did-christmas-become-so-commercial. Accessed 7 November 2019.

Kieren, Dianne. K., et al. "A Marker Method to Test a Phasing Hypothesis in Family Problem-Solving Interaction." *Journal of Marriage and the Family*, vol. 58, no. 2, 1996, pp. 442–455.

Lao-Tzu, "Quotation details." *The Quotations Page*, www.quotationspage.com/quote/24004. html. Accessed Accessed 8 November 2019.

McGoldrick, Monica, et al. *The Expanding Family Life Cycle: Individual, Family, and Social Perspectives.* 5th ed., Pearson, 2016.

Mind Tools. "What Are Your Values?" www.mindtools.com/pages/videos/values-transcript. htm. Accessed 8 November 2019

Morin, Amy. "Talking to Kids about Wants vs. Needs." *Very Well Family*, May 14, 2019, www.verywellfamily.com/how-to-talk-to-kids-about-wants-versus-needs-4150278. Accessed 22 Feb 2019

National Association of Investors. "Better Investing," www.betterinvesting.org/public/default. htm. Accessed 7 November 2019.

Nepal, Alto "Communication: Origin of the Word," 2011, nepalicommunication.blogspot. com/2011/01/origin-of-word.html. Accessed 7 November 2019.

Northwestern Mutual Life Insurance. "Planning and Progress Study 2018," www.northwest-ernmutual.com/planning-and-progress-2018. Accessed 23 Sept 2019

Olson, David.H. "Circumplex Model of Marital and Family Systems," *Journal of Family Therapy,* vol. 22, no. 2, 2000, pp. 144–167.

Olson, David. H. "Circumplex Model VII: Validation Studies and FACES III," *Family Process,* vol. 25, no. 3, 1986, pp. 337–351.

Olson, David H., Sprenkle, Douglas H., & Russell, Candyce S., "Circumplex Model of Marital and Family Systems I: Cohesion and Adaptability Dimensions, Family Types and Clinical Application," Family Process, vol. 18, no. 1: 1979, pp. 3-28.

Olson, David H., Russell, Candyce S., & Sprenkle, Douglas H., "Circumplex Model of Marital and Family Systems VI: Theoretical Update," Family Process, vol. 22, no. 1, 1983, pp. 69-83.

Olson, David H., et al. *Circumplex Model: Systemic Assessment and Treatment of Families.* Haworth, 1989.

Olson, David, H., McCubbin, Hamilton I., Barnes, Howard L., Larsen, Andrea S., Muxen, Marla J., & Wilson, Marc A. Families: What Makes Them Work (updated edition). Newbury Park, CA: Sage , 1989.

Pearson, Judy. C. *Communication in the Family: Seeking Satisfaction in Changing Times*. 3rd ed., Pearson, 1997.

Schrodt, Paul., et al. "A Social Relations Model of Everyday Talk and Relational Satisfaction in Stepfamilies." *Communication Monographs*, vol. 75, no. 2, 2008, pp. 190–217.

Shimanoff, Susan B. *Communication rules: Theory and research*. SAGE. 1980.

Soukup, Ruth. *31Days of Living Well and Spending Zero*. Life Well Lived, 2015.

Statler, US News and World Report Money, Do Prepaid 529 Plans Ever Make Sense? https://money.usnews.com/money/personal-finance/mutual-funds/articles/2014/09/03/do-prepaid-529-plans-ever-make-sense. Accessed 5 March 2019

Turner, Ralph. H. "Conflict and Harmony." *Family Interaction*, edited by Ralph H. Turner, Wiley, 1970, pp. 135–160.

U.S. Bureau of Labor Statistics. "Marriage and Divorce: Patterns by Gender, Race, and Educational Attainment," October 2013, www.bls.gov/opub/mlr/2013/article/marriage-and-divorce-patterns-by-gender-race-and-educational-attainment.html. Accessed 25 Sept 2019

U.S. Environmental Protection Agency. "Wasted Food Programs and Resources across the United States," www.epa.gov/sustainable-management-food/wasted-food-programs-and-resources-across-united-states. Accessed Accessed 8 November 2019.

University of Minnesota. "Twin Cities Student Budget," med.umn.edu/md-students/financial-aid/costs-budgeting/twin-cities-student-budget. Accessed 8 November 2019.

Vanguard. "Drafting Your Family Mission Statement," advisors.vanguard.com/iwe/pdf/FASGPCMS.pdf. Accessed 8 November 2019.

Verderber, K.S., Sellnow, D.D. & Verderber, R. F. *Communicate!* (15th ed.) Cengage. 2017.

Watzlawick, Paul, et al. *Pragmatics of Human Communication: a Study of Interactional Patterns, Pathologies, and Paradoxes*. W.W. Norton & Company, 2014.

Index